GW00802423

IRELAND AND HUNGARY

For two presidents

Mary McAleese and Árpád Göncz

Contents

Foreword

ÁRPÁD GÖNCZ

President of the Hungarian Republic

This is a book that will bring two nations, parallel in aspects of history, even closer together in spirit. In the penultimate chapter of *Ireland and Hungary*, Dr Thomas Kabdebo undertakes to solve the most arduous task: to acquaint Irish readers with the historic moment of 1956 (it was a historic moment lasting a mere two weeks) and make them feel the solemnity of the occasion. Irish readers were not part of the *56*, they were friendly onlookers with a special insight. As their country had often felt the *élan* of freedom fights they had a spiritual connection with a rising that had been suppressed, and its memory mourned. This book reflects the facts and spirit of revolutions the Irish reader will understand and will identify with.

While I was saying that writing about the revolution was an arduous task, it was, at the same time, a rewarding one too. Thomas Kabdebo, living in Hungary in 1956, was part of *56*, and his recall of the voices of the press gave such authenticity to his record of the events that I had a lump in my throat when I read it.

Here at home, in prison or out of it, we have had enough time to contemplate on the aftermath of *56*. When, fifteen years after the revolution, I managed to make a visit abroad I could surmise the meaning of *56*. After the war, which was known in the west in terms of Hungary being Germany's ally, *1956 redressed the balance*, placed Hungary back into European consciousness, and restored our country's honour. The fighters were those teenagers, mostly young workers, who fought against the Soviets, to their last breath, bearing all consequences: execution, or imprisonment, or exile. Abroad they were welcome and were given the chance to take their places in the society of their chosen country. Many have succeeded honourably, and many have been maintaining the spirit of 1956 which they represented. In terms of Ireland we can see the beginning of this process in the Irish welcome and in the practical help provided by the Irish branch of the Red Cross Society.

Those who are interested in the reality of 1956 – which spiritually connects with Irish freedom fights – will gain a true record from Thomas Kabdebo's book. I can personally vouch for its total integrity and authenticity.

Acknowledgments

My sincere thanks are due to the Royal Irish Academy and to the Department of Education for granting me a travel scholarship to Hungary in 1988 and in 1999 and to their administrators, Phil Barrett and Eithne O'Neill; to the Hungarian Ministry of Education and to the Hungarian Academy of Sciences and their emeritus librarian, Dr G. Rózsa; to the Széchényi Library and Mr Géza Poprády for receiving me as their guest; to Aidan O'Connor for his 'folder of 1956'; the readers and advisors of my original manuscript, Professor Donal Kerr, Professor James McGuire, Mr Seán Ó Luing, Dr Christopher Woods, Dr Keith Jeffery – even though I did not always accept their advice. Further thanks are due to the late Cardinal Tomás Ó Fiaich, Monsignor Mícheál Ledwith, Angela Long, Professor Richard Davies, Mr Hubert Mahony, the late Professor W.T. Moody, the late Professor Robin Dudley-Edwards, and the late Professor F.X. Martin for help and encouragement; to Mr Anthony O'Brien for letting me consult the O'Brien Diaries; and to those who helped in preparing or transcribing this script: Claire O'Beirne, Margaret O'Regan, Suzanne Redmond, Lily Kabdebo, Patrick Behan, Paula Leavy-McCarthy and Breege Lynch; and to Valerie Seymour for proof-reading my text. And this above all: I am grateful to my collaborators: Dr Jacqueline Hill, Mr Brian Maye and Dr Séamas Ó Síocháin, without whose help this volume would have been the poorer.

T.K.

Introduction

In this volume modest scholarship meets humble oratory; a Hungarian writer who is an emeritus Irish university librarian is assisted by three Irish scholars to home in on Irish-Hungarian affinities.

This is done through seven contributions. The first investigates Griffith's sources in an attempt to prove that his comparison was more than just nationalist propaganda, or a political programme for Ireland at the turn of the century. Then recalling the Irish and the Hungarian '1848' on the occasion of that revolutionary year's 150th anniversary, a short essay compares the predicaments of the two nations and their respective attempts to get out of the grip of a greater power.

The third and fourth essays of the volume deal with the Hungarian reception of contemporary Irish events: the Easter Rising, the later stages of Irish independence and Irish neutrality, both presented in the form of lectures to Hungarian university students.

The fifth piece concentrates on the Hungarian connexion with the two Roger Casements, father and son. Their fortunes were reported and commented upon in the Hungarian press between the wars.

Chapter six focuses on the Irish reaction to the Hungarian Rising of 1956: the reportage of the events, the Irish stance in the UN meetings in defence of Hungary, and the reception of Hungarian refugees in Ireland in November-December 1956.

The last section of this volume returns to Arthur Griffith in a more comprehensive yet essentially skeletal way. His bibliography is presented with a contextual addition of writing about the movement of which he was the motivator.

Ireland and Hungary is a study of parallels metaphorically 'all falling out of the cloak' of Arthur Griffith. There are hints that further 'affinities' (to do with *Weltanschaung*, temperament, social relations and cultural matters) have been interwoven into the fabric of historical 'similarities', and indeed, the extended topic would deserve a companion volume catering for all of these.

At the top level: after the cautious but amicable diplomatic contacts of the 1970s and 1980s, the 1990s saw the establishment of a Hungarian embassy in Dublin, followed by the creation of an Irish embassy in Budapest. The time between 1945 and 1989 saw a great social upheaval in Hungary. The country was colonised by the Soviet Union and the infrastructure of the society was atomised. Official contacts with so-called capitalists countries – and Ireland was one of them – were discouraged. This did not kill the positive sentiments of individual Hungarians or Irishmen. As soon as it was feasible – in the early 1990s – Irish-Hungarian and Hungarian-Irish Friendship Associations were formed. These complemented and complement the work of legations, presidential or ministerial visits and also the qualitative increase of single or reciprocal scholarships, and the flow in tourism. The trade links forged in the eighties (the Hungarian Chamber of Commerce; the Irish-Hungarian Economic Association) have been strengthened both in volume and in variety. Indeed, critics may say that trade is business which needs no affinities, only suitable goods to be exchanged. In a sense this is true, yet in another sense it is also true, that in the world of the internet choices, likings, sentiments, positive attitudes and sympathies vie with opportunities and with one another.

Historians are aware of the Irish emigration from the strictures of Cromwell in the seventeenth century, and indeed some Hungarian families of Irish origin trace the footsteps of their ancestors to those days. Three hundred years later there was an exodus from East to West. After the military defeat of the Hungarian revolution of 1956 some five hundred refugees were welcomed in Ireland. Those who stayed became Irish by nationality, their sons and daughters by sentiment too.

The affinities are lodged in the mind. These start with the ability to celebrate, to throw a party, to produce and enjoy instant merrymaking – an ability the Irish share with the Magyars. As their respective nationals are guaranteed of a good hearing, reciprocally, such musicians as the Chieftains and the Muzsikás Együttes move 'from home to home' when they visit the *other country* and are being received by the *other audiences*.

With the help of a world language, English, Irish literature is the top cultural export of Ireland. Given its linguistic isolation Magyar is less fortunate. Yet reciprocation and mutual appreciation is already a reality. Apart from the world of the theatre – obeying its own rules by the staging of a dozen Irish plays in the last fifteen years (and the same being also true of the radio) there have been three anthologies of Irish poetry in Hungary, and three 'focuses' on Hungarian verse in Irish journals. Besides such individual efforts as Michael Hartnett's translation of Ferenc Juhász's poetry into Irish, and Bill Tinley's translation of Olga Czilczer's prose poems into English, there has been a steady stream of Irish poets appearing in Hungarian translations: two volumes of Seamus Heaney, a collection of Des Egan's work in the journal *Nagyvilág* and many W.B. Yeats poems translated, as well as pieces by Thomas Kinsella, Brendan Kennelly and many others.

The Irish and the Hungarians have yet to discover each other's fairytales - known, so far, only to the *cognoscenti*. It will be a revelation to see how free phantasy moves in Ireland, and in Magyarland, and what parallels the tales will offer.

And at last but not least: this volume is not only *about* affinities; it is also the *product* of affinities – joint scholarships for research, two opportunities to deliver lectures and three Irish academics to help a Hungarian.

PART ONE

The Hungarian-Irish 'parallel' and Arthur Griffith's use of his sources

> I have heard it sung,
> it may be true or no,
> that Lawrence Tar down into hell did go.
> And there he saw prepared a fiery bed,
> four fiery men stood at the foot and head.[1]

The above stanza goes back to the earliest references of a Hungarian visiting Ireland. Lörinc Tar, a Hungarian cleric writing at the time of Emperor Sigismund, visited St Patrick's Purgatory in Lough Derg and wrote a medieval account of his journey in Latin, somewhat in the style of St Brendan's voyage, in other words mixing legend with travelogue, real with imaginary description, religious experience with politico-religious exhortation. The point of Tar's report from hell was that, having gained access to it through St Patrick's Purgatory, he spotted the emperor being roasted there and was now anxious to warn him to mend his ways. This Latin tale or vision was known to the sixteenth-century popular soldier-poet Sebestyén Tinódi, who wrote, at about 1550, the *Chronicle of Sigismund*[2] which revived Tar's journey and his vision.

From 1655 to 1663 Walter Lynch, bishop of Clonfert, who had been made a fugitive by Cromwell's troops, stayed in the town of Győr in the west of Hungary, leaving an image of the Holy Virgin as a gift to the cathedral. It had

---

1 'The Chronicle of Sigismund', translated by Michael Beevor in Thomas Kabdebo and Paul Tabori (eds.), *The poetry of Hungary* (Chicago, 1976), vol. 1, pt. 1, p. 49. According to Joseph Szövérffy, 'St Patrick's Purgatory and the Hungarians', in *Hungarian Quarterly*, 1962, vol. 3, pp. 115-32, a certain knight called George was the first Hungarian visitor in 1353. 2 Sigismund of Luxembourg, 1387-1437, king of Hungary. There were other fragmentary Hungarian references to the 'Purgatory': visio Tnugdeli, Sándor Kodex, which refers to 'Marcus's work of 1150.' János Horváth, *A magyar irodalmi müveltseg kezdetei* (Budapest, 1931), p. 199. Horváth is probably mistaken. The Tractatus de Purgatorio sancti Patricii was written by H. of Saltrey, a Cistercian monk, between 1179 and 1184: J.-M. Picard and Y. de Pontfarcy, *Saint Patrick's Purgatory* (Dublin 1985).

been revered through the centuries as the 'Virgin that shed tears' on St Patrick's day in 1697, and was shown in 1985 to His Eminence Cardinal Tomás Ó Fiaich on his visit to Hungary as he subsequently related to the present writer. This was confirmed, in a letter to the present writer, by Dr Kornél Pataky, bishop of Györ, dated 23 March 1988, who enclosed a reproduction of the painting.

Medieval Hungary was almost equivalent, territorially, with the Danubian basin and was predominantly Catholic. Roughly coinciding in time with the advance of the Reformation, the Turks split Hungary into three: the kingdom of Hungary, recognising the Habsburgs as their king in the west, Hungary under Turkish conquest in the middle, and semi-independent Transylvania ruled by a Hungarian prince under Turkish suzerainty. In the West people remained predominantly Catholic, in the East they became mostly Protestant, and in the middle they were both – in the words of later historians: *cuius regio, eius religio*.[3]

Depending on their religion, Hungarian historians of the seventeenth century looked upon the plight of Ireland with sympathy, in as much as Irish events were mentioned or chronicled by them. But this was, of course, a rough and ready measure in a world where political alliances were as topsy turvey as individual fortunes or loyalties.[4] Thus it could happen that, writing at the beginning of the eighteenth century, the Protestant Mihály Cserei found himself on the side of the Catholic Habsburg king who happened to be in alliance with England against the France of Louis XIV. Cserei wrote in 1708: 'The French king stealthily conspired with the nobility in Hybernia as they, being all papists, were all annoyed with the rule of Protestant English kings, wishing to have the dux de Vallis[5] as their own ruler …'

The idea of a parallel fate of Hungary and Ireland was first hinted at by Prince Ferenc Rákóczi II, who found himself in secret alliance with Louis XIV in trying to liberate Hungary from Habsburg rule. He had witnessed the end of the Turkish rule in Hungary (1688), the absorption of semi-independent Transylvania into the Austrian empire, and the beginning of an absolutist regime in Hungary now 'reconquered' by the empire. Rákóczi's war of liberation (1703–11) was less a clash of regular armies and more a guerrilla war. 'Since Caesar fought against the Gauls I think hardly any such war was waged as this … I discovered the spirit of the Gauls in (my) Hungarians.'[6]

3 Bálint Homan and Gyula Szekfü, *Magyar történet* (Budapest, 1939), vol. 4, p. 585.   4 The Catholic approach: P.F. Aug. Maria Rosner, *Servitus Mariana Albpiciis Austriacis in Germaniae, Hungariae et Boemiae regne reparata* (Vienna, 1677), as against the Protestant approach: Mihály Cserei, *Erdély históriája* (1661-1711), (New edition, Budapest, 1983).   5 Dux de Vallis = Prince of Wales, i.e. the Pretender James III. Ibid. p. 408. (N.B. Unless otherwise mentioned all Hungarian language excerpts were translated by the present writer.)   6 Rákóczi, Ferenc, II *Emlékiratok* (Budapest, 1979), p. 305.

At the height of his success, in 1707, Rákóczi dethroned the house of Habsburg. Although he did not take the crown of Hungary and was content with the title of ruler, the dethroning of the Habsburgs was seen by him to be an act similar to the Stuart restoration that had been attempted in Ireland.[7]

It had been in France's interest to create diversions against England: in Hungary to aid the Magyar insurgents against their Habsburg king who was an ally of the English; in Ireland to help those who would use any means to get rid of the English yoke; so French diplomacy had recognised and tried to exploit 'a parallel' albeit asynchronically.

Rákóczi's attempt at re-establishing Hungarian liberty ended in exile, military defeat and a social-economic compromise favourable to Austria. But the colonial status of Hungary (1688-1703) had, as a result of the upheaval, given way to a semi-colonial epoch (1712-1847).

O'Connell's figure loomed large at the beginning of the nineteenth century all over Europe, including Hungary. Hungarian language and literature, revitalised, saw the publication of new literary and political organs and the best of them could hardly fail to describe, comment upon and/or uphold O'Connell's achievements. Thus, we find an account of his parliamentary exploits in the 1835 issue of the *Regélö* (Chronicler), a tribute to him in the 26 March 1837 issue of the *Atheneum*, which describes him as a great patriot, the leader of Ireland's fight for independence, and multiple references in the 1843 issues of Kossuth's *Pesti Hirlap*.[8]

In the autumn of 1843 J.A. Blackwell, a diplomatic agent of the British government in Hungary (a Catholic of Scottish descent, 1798-1886) reported to his superiors in Vienna that the archbishop of Esztergom quizzed him about Ireland. Kopácsy was much concerned about the famine and asked if Blackwell had any hope for a way out. Blackwell answered that population in Ireland grew faster than jobs and even without the famine the Irish would have had to emigrate. He more or less equated O'Connell with Kossuth and said that both had been agitating for revolutionary measures.[9]

This opinion was echoed and reinforced in 1844 by Sir Robert Gordon, the British ambassador in Vienna, who wrote to his brother, the earl of Aberdeen,

---

7 *Universis orbis Christiani* (a patent to the Christian world) (Löcse, 1707). Rákóczi asserted that Hungary's connection with Austria was of the same nature as Scotland is with England, whereas Austria wanted to treat Hungary as England treated Ireland, as a conquered country, without, however, ever having conquered it. Ladislas Hengelmuller, *Hungary's first for national existence* (London, 1913) pp. 111-200, who was one of Griffith's sources when updating his second edition of the *Resurrection*, to construct the third.   8 Gyula Kókay, *A magyar sajtó története* (Budapest, 1979), pp. 458, 509, 675.   9 Cardinal József Kopácsy (1775-1847). Thomas Kabdebo, 'A.J. Blackwell' (Manchester University doctoral thesis 1983), pp. 143-4. (It must be said that Blackwell was eventually 'won over' to the Hungarian cause, quarrelled with his superiors in the Foreign Office and was finally dismissed.)

the British foreign secretary: the members of the Védegylet (Protective Association) are sworn, and a rent is collected, from which Kossuth is to derive a handsome maintenance. O'Connell's Repeal Association is professed to be a model for the proceedings of these *soi-disant* Hungarian patriots.[10]

Indeed, by the mid-forties the Hungarian reading public was no stranger to the special plight of Ireland. In 1837 two of the country's leading nationalist[11] politicians, Bertalan Szemere[12] and Ferenc Pulszky,[13] had visited Ireland separately, and in their travelogues gave an account of their experience. They both crossed from the Clyde and stayed in Dublin, but only Pulszky came via Douglas and went to see beauty spots, such as Glendalough, the Giant's Causeway and Dunluce Castle. They were both appalled by the poverty and hunger, and both were aware of the strength and extent of political agitation in Ireland. 'My heart pounded as I came to visit a *sick country*,' wrote Szemere (p. 187). He climbed Nelson's column for an overview but descending he nearly fainted at the sight of misery. Szemere did not hesitate to lay the blame at Britain's door: 'whatever horrible rags there are in Britain are brought over here as if in exchange for the crop which they extort from the hungry population'. Szemere visited a workhouse and called Dublin a 'city of paupers'. His heart went out to the Irish: 'these optimistic, good humoured, gregarious people who do not have half as many prejudices as the English or the Scots'. At the end of his account Szemere analysed the causes of poverty and hunger as follows: political slavery, payment of tithes to the Church of Ireland, making potato a general, almost exclusive staple crop, population growth, land tenure, the lack of native industry and commerce.

The third contemporary study, *Poverty in Ireland* (Pest, 1840), was published by Baron József Eötvös, a friend of Pulszky and Szemere who made the experiences of his friends a starting point to study the causes and effects of poverty.

The year 1848 is a European watershed. All the great empires experience a revolutionary upsurge that culminates in a series of cataclysmic revolutions. At the eastmost point the Hungarian revolution was extended and transformed into a protracted freedom fight; the furthest point in the West saw the insurrection by the Young Irelanders, William Smith O'Brien and his followers, the spiritual

10 Gordon to Aberdeen, Vienna, 19 November 1844, PRO FO 7. 131. Ibid. p. 195.   11 Nationalist in the Hungarian context is used to denote a person working for the cause of Hungarian independence. Politicians opposing the tactics of the Austrian government called themselves 'the Opposition,' although there had been no opposition party in the Parliament until March 1847. After that date and up to independence in March 1848 the Party of the Austrian government was the 'Conservatives' the opposition the 'Progressives'.   12 Bertalan Szemere, *Utazás Külföldön* (Pest, 1840), pp. 185-97. (Szemere became prime minister in 1849.)   13 Pulszky, *Aus dem Tagebuch eines in Grossbritannien reisenden Ungarn* (Pest, 1837), pp. 125-38. Pulszky became Foreign Minister in 1848.

ancestors of 1916. The protagonists of the Irish aftermath of 1848, Michael Doheny, John Mitchel and William Smith O'Brien, each in his own way 'discovered' for himself – and through their journals, correspondence and agitation discovered it for others too – that there was a similarity between the 'Hungarian cause' and the Irish struggle.[14] These names need no introduction; their aspirations and activities need no detailed descriptions for students of Irish history. But some apposite points may be made of their personal fortunes as their situations became an integral part of their political fate. Men discover national parallels when they see the similarity of circumstance and feel the tinge of kindred afflictions on their own skin.

The failure of the insurrection in 1848 rendered Michael Doheny – formerly a prosperous lawyer – a fugitive who then went to America and became co-founder of the Fenian Brotherhood. In his classic work *The Felon's Track* (a book 'embracing the leading events in the Irish struggle from the year 1843 to the close of 1848') Doheny described the critical days in July 1848 in Kilkenny thus: 'the ground once chosen by a great general for its natural capabilities may safely be chosen again, and usually is, as in Hungary, for instance. The very posts and battlefields held and fought by Bem and Dembinski were the same whereon Huniad and Corvinus, four and five hundred years ago, fought against the Turks and Bosmans. Thus we had the sanction of a great example ... '[15]

Although Doheny's statement was more or less true when considering Hungarian geography, it was still remarkable in two respects: it noticed that a successful stand against an enemy can be gained on home ground if the ground is well chosen, and it revealed that Doheny (and presumable his likeminded compatriots) had a more than casual knowledge of Hungarian events. With hindsight one might be tempted to say that the Young Irelanders after 1848 were almost approaching the idea, 'Take your stand like the Hungarians did', but this was not yet the case; there is rarely a case for such symbolic statements until one

---

14 The emergence of Irish nationalism - or shall we say, re-emergence, for the 'patriots' of the 18th century were, in fact proto-nationalists, before the term was coined in the late 1790s - coincided with English nationalism of the 'renewed' type. Moreover, as far as cross-channel or overseas territories were concerned English nationalism was wrapped into 'British' nationalism, perhaps a larger 'territorial' variety of this upsurge. The clash was, therefore, not only inevitable, but the harshness of the victor over the vanquished could almost be taken for granted; cf: George Newman, *The rise of English nationalism* (London, 1987) pp. 160-3.   15 Doheny finished his Ms. in New York on 20 September 1849 very shortly after the surrender at Világos on 13 August 1849 when Arthur Görgey (1818-1916) at the head of the main Hungarian army laid down his arms to the invading Russians. Huniad = János Hunyadi, governor of Hungary (1407-1456); Corvinus = Matthias Corvinus, Hunyadi's son, king of Hungary (1443-90); József Bem (1794-1850) was a Polish revolutionary and Hungarian general; Henryk Dembinski (1791-1864) was Polish insurgent and Hungarian general. For the quotation see the reissue of the original edition: Michael Doheny, *The felon's track* (Dublin, 1914), p. 296.

can point to a successful conclusion, and in 1849 and right through to the late 1850s Hungary was once again in shackles. But Irish contemporaries could certainly see this much: that Hungary had a long war of liberation which was only crushed by the combined might of Austria and Russia; and that just as they, the Young Irelanders, refugees of 1848, proto-Fenians and other patriots – turned into felons – were scattered around the globe, the Hungarians of 1848 fled the reprisals and were scattered too; just as the Irish upheld the cause of an independent Ireland, the Hungarians, too, were doing their best to regain Hungarian liberty. In John Mitchel's words, 'the Austrians are hanging and shooting general officers. Kossuth, the immortal governor, and Bem, the fine old general, are refugees in Turkey, other Hungarians and Poles flying to the United States. Justice and right everywhere buried in blood.'[16]

Mitchel, arrested in May 1848, was tried and sentenced to transportation for fourteen years. At the time of writing, in 1850, he was at the Cape of Good Hope feeling a special empathy for Kossuth, who was then in exile in Kiutahia, Turkey.[17] In the summer of 1851 Kossuth was freed and made his way to America – via England – where he was to collect money for the Hungarian cause in general and for a campaign to liberate Hungary by armed insurrection in particular. Mitchel, according to his *Jail Journal* (pp. 148, 205, 288-92, 355-6, 441-2, 454-8) followed his fortune avidly.

Another Young Irelander, free at the time, interviewed Kossuth in New York in the early spring of 1852. He was Thomas Devin Reilly, who gave a detailed account of his meeting with Kossuth in a letter to Mitchel, dated 24 April 1852, which Mitchel quotes extensively in his book. Apart from the humorous asides and multiple exchange of views (the Young Irelander did not approve of Kossuth turning for help to all and sundry, namely to English liberals),[18] Reilly reported to Mitchel: 'I wished at all events to assure him of the deep sympathy and

16 John Mitchel, *Jail journal* (Dublin, 1913) p. 205. Note that a contemporary, Thomas Davis, wrote in a similar vein in the early 1840s: 'And Austria on Italy –/the Roman eagle chained/Bohemia, Servia, Hungary,/within her cluthes gasp;/And Ireland struggles gallantly/in England's loosening grasp': *Thomas Davis*, ed. by Arthur Griffith (Dublin 1914), p. 73.   17 Kossuth, Louis (1804-1894) – Minister of Finance in the Hungarian Government, restored chiefly through his exertions in 1848. When Austria treacherously attacked Hungary in that year, Kossuth took charge of the national defences. When Austria called in the Russians, Kossuth replied by a decree separating Hungary and Austria. After the defeat of his country he fled to Turkey and then visited France, England and America. He died in Turin. Of the extensive literature referring to Kossuth's activities some of the definitive works are: Lajos Kossuth, *Memories of my exile* (London, 1880); Dénes Jánossy: *A Kossuth emigráció Angliában és Amerikában* 2 vols. (Budapest, 1940-48). It should be noted further that K.F. Hennigsen – an expatriate Irishman and a Liberal MP – was one of Kossuth's most ardent helpers in Turkey. Griffith would have read Kossuth's memoirs in the National Library. 18 Engels too criticised Kossuth in 1851 for being, like St Paul, 'all things to all men.' (*Marx-Engels Werke*, Berlin, 1960–, vol. 27, pp. 368-9).   19 Mitchel, *Jail Journal*, p. 290.

affection of all Irish republicans.' To which Mitchel added: 'I can fancy these two interlocutors ... I wish I had been there to make a trio.'[19] In his soliloquy it occurred to Mitchel too that Kossuth whom he had humorously described as a 'Kalmuck' or a 'tartar' was an O'Connell-type figure.[20]

While Kossuth and the Hungarian exiles extended their agitation to the continent of Europe, forming a directorate (L. Kossuth, Count L. Teleki, General G. Klapka) which concluded a secret diplomatic agreement with Napoleon III and Count Cavour, to liberate the country with outside help, Hungarian politicians at home successfully conducted a policy of 'passive resistance' to the Austrian administration. This took the form of withholding payment of taxes, refusal of administrative posts and – above all – non-participation in the imperial parliament. The Italian-Austrian war of 1859, in which Italy was aided by France, ended with the defeat of the imperial troops of Austria, most of whose large Hungarian contingent obeyed the directorate's manifesto and became deserters. Nonetheless, the planned intervention did not take place – partly, because the French did not wish to invest more money or troops, but mainly because Hungarian public opinion of 1859 listened more to the pacifying voice of Ferenc Deák than to the warlike call of Kossuth. In October 1860 Emperor Francis Joseph issued a patent which opened the door to the restoration of constitutional rights. A parliament was called in Pest for the summer of 1861 and (for the first time after twelve years of repression) a dialogue started between the Hungarian parliament and the king.

This was when William Smith O'Brien, the exiled leader of the Young Irelanders, decided to visit Hungary.[21] O'Brien had been arrested on 15 August 1848 and was sentenced to be hanged, drawn and quartered. Early in 1849 Queen Victoria ordered the sentence of death to be commuted to transportation for life. In the summer of that year O'Brien was sent to Tasmania. While John Mitchel eventually escaped from Tasmania, O'Brien remained there until a pardon was granted to him in 1854. In that year he returned to Europe, staying in Brussels for two years, and then he re-settled in Ireland in 1856. In 1859 he made a voyage to America; in 1861 to Germany, Austria and – through Hungary – to Poland. Presumably because the condition of his return to Irish soil was a promise of non-involvement in politics, O'Brien never attempted to publish his travel journals,[22] which would have shown

---

20 The Reverend Sidney Smith, a well known wit of Victorian English society (whose comparison between Ireland and Hungary became the motto of Griffith's *Resurrection of Hungary – a parallel for Ireland*), was not unequivocal in his praise of O'Connell: 'he, it cannot be denied, has done a great deal for Ireland, and, on the whole, I believe 'he meant well, but "hell" as Johnson says, "is paved with good intentions"' (Sidney Smith, *A memoir of the Reverend Sidney Smith*, London, 1885, 2 vols., p. 390).   21 W.S. O'Brien (1803-64) left a dozen unpublished travel journals to his descendants, often referred to as 'Diaries.'   22 The Diaries are now in the possession of Anthony O'Brien of Dublin, his descendant, who kindly permitted me to read and copy the two notebooks that cover his ancestor's stay in Hungary. I am also indebted to Professor Richard Davis of the University of Tasmania for calling my attention to the existence of this valuable Ms material.

his unwavering commitment to the cause of Irish independence. The journals of his Hungarian visit cover three weeks from 14 August 1861, when he arrived at Pest by steamboat, to 8 September when he left the castle of Hotkócz in the north of Hungary and crossed the Polish border by coach.[23]

Passing through Vienna, O'Brien noted there the absence of Hungarian delegates in the imperial parliament. He then decided to visit the Hungarian diet/parliament, still in session in Pest, in order to learn more of the stand and tactics of its members. From the galleries and in the company of good interpreters he listened spellbound while Deák declared: 'the Diet, being unable to act except upon the basis of the Hungarian Constitution, has neglected nothing to establish that basis and to guarantee it completely. The elections prescribed by law to complete the Diet, the re-establishment of a responsible ministry and of the laws which had been suspended, were, above all, necessary in order that the Diet might engage in the discussion of the projects of law. Towards that end our efforts have been directed; but our reiterated addresses have been without result ... we enter our solemn protest and we declare that we are seriously attached to all our laws and consequently to the laws sanctioned in 1848 which no Diet has modified and that we regard every measure taken by the government in opposition to those laws as hostile to the constitution.'[24]

'It was the best day of my life', reported O'Brien in his journal, having witnessed the debate and discussed with the Hungarians the implications of their stand. In the eight days prior to attending the parliamentary debates in Pest, O'Brien discussed with Hungarian landowners the tactics of 'passive resistance' to direct Austrian rule without parliament; the measures adopted; the Austrian government's counter-measures; the laws of 1848 which had been sanctioned by the king in 1848 but revoked; the beginning of an independent Hungarian government; and the rights of a Hungarian parliament. Leaving Pest for the country immediately after the dissolution of the resolute parliament, O'Brien readily drew the conclusion that Griffith was to draw again forty-three years later: *Ireland must have its own parliament.*[25]

23 Count Béla Széchenyi, son of the great reformer István Széchenyi was, for the first part of his stay, O'Brien's guide.   24 W.S. O'Brien's Diary. Deák's speech was reported internationally, in *The Times* and *Freeman's Journal* (28 Aug. 1861), and in many other European papers.   25 W.S. O'Brien's Diary, 14 Aug. to 8 Sept. 1861. O'Brien is quite lyrical about the Hungarian countryside and informative about the religious tolerance that existed in Hungary. He met a variety of people – for instance, the mayor and burghers of Debrecen, coach drivers, tradesmen on the journey and clergymen. He described how at the height of patriotic feeling the Hungarians recited the words and sung the tune of the poem 'Appeal' by Mihály Vörösmarty. He meticulously recorded four versions of this ode in his notebook: the Hungarian original together with its English, German and French translation. In the last days of August O'Brien met Deák in the Pest City Park. They talked through an interpreter because, although O'Brien understood German, he was hesitant to speak it. Later on he discovered he could communicate in Latin with educated Hungarians.

In the next six years, matters social, economic and legal eased up considerably between Austria and Hungary. For its economic survival the monarchy needed the surplus food products grown in Hungary, and for its economic growth Hungary welcomed capital investment from Austria. In 1866 Austria was challenged by Prussia for its German hegemony and 'the Solferino of 1859' was repeated in Könniggrätz, where the Austrians were routed. This defeat and the Hungarian constitutional resistance were the basis of the Compromise concluded in 1867 between Baron von Beust, the Austrian chancellor, representing his emperor, and the Hungarian delegation led by the one-time exile and future prime minister, Count G. Andrássy. The architect of the Compromise, Ferenc Deák, remained in the background. The Compromise created a new form of state, the Austro-Hungarian monarchy, in which the emperor of Austria and the king of Hungary were one person – hence a personal union – dispensing separate functions. Separate legislatures, parliaments, ministries (albeit some were combined) made it possible for a separate crowning of the king, separate but intertwined economic institutions, etc. From a downtrodden nation Hungary became a partner.

The *Freeman's Journal* faithfully reported every factual turn of this saga. On 25 September 1867, for instance, its readers learnt about the bill sanctioning new railways in Hungary; five days later it reported the protocol that was to conclude financial arrangements between the two signatories of the Compromise. The issues for 6 and 7 November gave short accounts of the debate on apportioning the share of the new monarchy's inherited debt.

But the issue for 1 November also reported on Fenianism, a matter close to the heart of the Young Ireland survivors. The paper had, indeed, been reporting on the Fenian trials in May (the issues for 14, 27, 29 May in particular) giving rise to a number of letters and expressions of public sympathy on behalf of Thomas Burke and Patrick Doran. The sympathisers included the poet and journalist John Francis O'Donnell,[26] who composed his poem, '*Cui bono*', to ask a challenging question: 'Is it, was it worthwhile to risk your life for the cause of independent Ireland?' We shall quote a few poignant stanzas from the long poem to illustrate O'Donnell's ideas:

Cui bono

They failed, I grant you – Klapka failed
But not the cause for which he bled;

---

26 John Francis O'Donnell (1837-74) writer of ballads, one of the editors of *The Nation*. '*Cui bono*' first appeared posthumously in O'Donnell's books of verse, entitled *Poems* (London, 1891). It was almost certainly composed in 1867. Griffith republished the ballad in his sequence of *Irish ballads* that appeared under one of his pseudonyms 'Cuguan.'

Disaster, blood, and tears entrailed,
Till beaten Hungary ran red ...

But still the mighty Magyar race,
Persisting, won the doubtful day;
The empire, charmed to sudden grace
Achieved its mission – forced its way ...

Are we unworthy less renown?
Are we unworthy less reward?
We who, despite our master's frown,
Cling to tradition of the sword ...

I say – let history answer this –
For us, we freely risk the chance ...
To ladies, whispered voice and kiss;
For freedom, rifle, sword, and lance ...

From the above it is obvious that the poet celebrates the Hungarian constitutional victory and urges Irishmen to fight on, despite setbacks, finally to overcome the foe. Furthermore it is also clear that the poet attributes a large share of the Hungarian victory to those who have fought on the battlefields. He implies that the violent struggle contributed to the eventual Hungarian victory and the same seemed unavailable for the Irish. Whether one agrees with their view or not, there can be no doubt that the two arms of the Hungarian struggle as personified by Kossuth, who resorted to arms, and Deák, who used passive resistance, expressed the two sides of the Hungarian national character, or, to put it less abstractly, the very same people were capable of different outlets: counter aggression or unified, peaceful resistance.

How did Arthur Griffith discover – or rather rediscover – the 'Hungarian parallel' as a recipe for Irish independence?[27] *The Resurrection of Hungary* was first published in the pages of the *United Irishman* in 1904, then brought out,

---

27 Cf. Warwick Gould, 'How Ferencz Renyi spoke up', *Yeats Annual* 3 (1985) 199-205 gives an account of a poem by Yeats: *How Ferencz Renyi kept silent* published by Griffith on p. 2 of the 24 December 1903 issue of *United Irishman*, with its preceding and subsequent history. Griffith's point was that Yeats did write a poem describing a Hungarian hero, an example for the Irish, which had not been anthologised. This poem, was prefaced with a stanza: 'We, too, have seen our bravest and our best/To prison go, and mossy ruin rest/Where homes once whitened vale and mountain crest,/Therefore, O nation of the bleeding breast,/Libations from the Hungary of the West!' This connection was also known to the Hungarian scholar Dr Ferenc Molnár of Kossuth University, Debrecen.

unaltered, in pamphlet form in the same year, achieving an unaltered second edition, and in 1918 published in a modified third edition.

As soon as the first edition was out, reactions, critical, encouraging and cautious, began to urge its author to expand on the methodology blueprinted in the work, and Griffith was inspired to call the first, 'the non-violent' Sinn Fein to life, expand on his economic strategies, advance to the forefront of the Irish political arena, suffer imprisonment as an 'ideologist' – for he had no direct part in the 1916 rising – and, just before elected to represent Ireland in negotiations, improve on the blueprint.

Some apologists of *The Resurrection* argue that it was not accurate historically, its argument being *more symbolic* than factually based.[28] A more recent writer argued that Griffith's approach to Irish history was essentially no different from his approach to the history of Hungary: 'he hitched on to a few issues and gave them a particular significance...'[29]

We propose to re-examine *The Resurrection of Hungary* by uncovering some of its sources and checking the authenticity of its statements, not just contrasting the main events but demonstrating the dynamics of Hungarian history to which it refers. Historical veracity of parallels – even critics would allow – that does not depend on the minutiae of chronological, social, institutional or even economic details but on the similarity of situations. Parallels are drawn by active agents of the historical process who discover similar agents acting in a similar historical process. In that sense parallels are always discovered against not dissimilar backgrounds, in situations fairly akin, such as: 'method of rule', 'dependency', 'empire building', 'colonising' or 'being colonised'. But, perhaps, the most relevant is the correlation of contexts: emerging nationalism, nationalism in its assertive phase, or, the fight for the survival of, or even for the dominance of the same religion, could bring two geographically distant countries into a valid parallel. The 'closer' the context, the 'better' the parallel.

How did Griffith discover the parallel? There were, as we have seen, a number of precursors before him, some on the Hungarian, others on the Irish side, as well as quasi-independent observers, who were ready to draw comparisons,

28 Such criticism was voiced in the *Irish Times* by Thomas Woods, writing under the pseudonym of Thomas Hogan, and even by Padraig Colum, who considered that Griffith's parallel was more symbolic than real. On the other hand, Kuno Meyer, the philologist, wrote in *An Claidheamh Soluis* on 3 December 1904: 'Nor can it be denied that the victorious struggle of the Hungarians for their national existence affords many lessons which may usefully serve the cause of an Irish Ireland. A series of brilliantly-written and instructive articles on the recent history of Hungary in the columns of the *United Irishman* has but lately drawn the attention of its readers to the subject.' (I thank Sean O Luing for bringing this to my attention.) Some of the early critics such as Tom Kelly were eventually won over to the side of Griffith and his close supporters, like Edward Martyn and Alderman Walter C. Cole.   29 Donal McCartney, 'The political use of history in the work of Arthur Griffith, in *Journal of Contemporary History* 8/1 (1973) 10.

between the situation of the two countries or between certain leaders of either countries. But to have a *parallel*[30] it is necessary to discover multiple similarities to have a nearly matching context[31] and (since drawing a parallel is an exercise that must result in an intellectual product) an underlying purpose as well. Griffith had been in South Africa for several years and returned to Ireland in 1898.[32] The years in Transvaal were, for Griffith, a time of self-searching and reflection, a period of alternative activity after the disruption of the nationalist rank following the fall of Parnell. Griffith had had an ambivalent attitude: he admired Parnell to the end but was dissatisfied with the limits of the home rule movement.

In 1897 he met 'a magnificent Magyar' in the Transvaal. He recalled the incident in the pages of the *United Irishman*, 28 April 1900: 'I taught the ignorant the Kafir language ... and he went round to the Zulu cookboy and remarked: 'I am an idiot of seven generations.' The cookboy grinned and said, 'Yes, yes, master.' The ignorant discovered my perfidy and swore by Kossuth and Görgey and Bem – he was a magnificent Magyar – that I should die. I purchased my life from him for a cigar ... and we swore eternal friendship.'[33] Thus Griffith's Hungarian commitment started with a joke. Justice Lennon, in the notes to his typescript, 'Griffith of Dublin', remarked that there was evidence that Griffith had been looking at Irish and English newspapers, in 1901, to uncover leading articles on Hungary, and that Griffith was reading John Mitchel's *Jail Journal* with its references to the Hungarian struggle of 1848-9. Among other associations, Griffith had been a member of the Young Ireland Society before he left for the Transvaal, and on his return founded, with William Rooney, the *United Irishman*. The very choice of these names recalls the times and aspirations of the Irish 1848 movement which, as we have seen, had found a spiritual link with the Hungarian struggle of 1848-9 and its aftermath.

30 Cultural anthropology knows its own version of 'parallelism': 'a similarity between the evolution and achievements of two different cultures' (*Oxford English Dictionary*, Suppt. Oxford, 1982, vol. 3, p. 262).   For the comparisons and parallels of nationalism see: John Breuilly, *Nationalism and the state* (Manchester, 1982), p. 92, who refers to both Hungarian and Irish nationalism as 'separatist nationalism in the nineteenth century.'   31 Apart from those already mentioned parallels we can list Isaac Butt, and W.E. Gladstone on the introduction of the Home Rule bill in 1886, and Gladstone's writing to Lord Acton in 1888, in *Selections from the correspondence of the first Lord Acton* (London, 1917), p. 190.   32 *DNB* 1922-1930, pp. 364-7.   33 The incident is hinted at by both: Padraig Colum, *Arthur Griffith* (Dublin, 1959), p. 44 and by M.J. Lennon, 'Griffith of Dublin' (National Library Typescript, no. 781, no date).   Justice Lennon left his typescript and the notes to this typescript to the National Library. (I obtained, for the Maynooth Griffith Archives, a ms. copy of this.) The notes are exercise book pages that list references of Hungarian and other topics in Griffith's writings, year by year. These are matched up by added remarks, from Lennon to events reported in given years. Lennon analysed the *United Irishman* prior to the publication of *The Resurrection*, but some of Lennon's notes seem to have been misplaced (or never acquired?) so we do not have a consistent, chronological set.

It looks fairly certain that Griffith never read William Smith O'Brien's *Travel Journal*, which drew a near lesson for Ireland from Hungary's constitutional stand, as Griffith never referred to O'Brien in this context. But it is quite possible that, in his effort to scour the newspapers of the past for reports on Hungary, he came across two articles in the *Freeman's Journal*, the first written by 'W' and published on 26 May 1860, the second by 'Eta' published on 4 August 1866. The first was actually entitled 'Ireland and Hungary: a parallel' and stated that the suppression of the Irish constitution in 1849 paralleled the suppression of the Irish constitution by the act of union.[34] The second, entitled 'A lesson from Hungary', claimed that Deák's demands were similar to those of the Irish patriots of 1782, so it was Ireland's turn to put forward demands similar to Deák's. Some sixteen years later, Deák's death was reported in the world press[35] – a fact known to Griffith. He may or may not have come across the Deák obituary in the 12 February issue of the *Irish World* (New York) which, among other tributes, reported sending a message of condolences to Budapest by the Irish Association, which said that Deák was 'an eternal example of the power of nationality against foreign aggression'.

With different emphasis and varying detail, all Griffith's biographers agree that on his return from South Africa he studied the politics of Central Europe and was 'fascinated by the struggle of the Hungarians'.[36] As early as 1899 Griffith wrote an article, under the pseudonym of 'Nationalist' in which he contemplated setting up a 'National Organisation' along the lines that Kossuth had done in the early 1840s in Hungary, his final comment being: 'not Deák but Kossuth was the real winner of even the semi-independence of Hungary'.[37]

In 1900 a new association, Cumann na nGaedheal, was formed which remained comparatively unimportant until its 1902 convention, when the Cork resolution – calling on Irish Americans to show defiance of England by repudiating the parliamentary policy of nationalist leaders – attracted attention. Moreover, Griffith proposed an amendment which called on Americans to withhold support until such time as the Irish party took up the intrepid policy of the Hungarian parliament of 1861.[38] The amendment was passed. Griffith's speech which followed the lines of the amended resolution cited the example of Hungary who would negotiate with Austria 'only as one independent nation with another'.[39] Griffith referred to Hungarian self-confidence and self-education, inviting all Irishmen to follow its example.

34 For this piece of research and several subsequent observations I am indebted to Mr Hubert Mahony who before switching professions had done very good groundwork on Griffith.   35 *Annual Register* (London, 1876), pp. 190–2; *The Times*, 28 January, 1876.   36 Calton Younger, *Arthur Griffith* (Dublin, 1981), p. 22.   37 *United Irishman*, 29 April 1899.   38 Lennon, op. cit., p. 10; F.L.S. Lyons, *John Dillon* (London, 1968), pp. 224–7.

Three weeks after the Convention, Griffith wrote an editorial in the *United Irishman* in which he said that Austrian rule after 1849 offered a striking parallel to English rule in Ireland since the Union. Hungary, under the leadership of Kossuth and Deák, won semi-independence. Kossuth was a separatist; Deák demanded equal partnership. In 1861 Austria was unsuccessful in trying to introduce a type of 'home rule', and in 1867 Hungary had her own parliament, government, king. This was the lesson Ireland had to learn.[40] For Griffith this lesson included that Ireland should not face England in arms. But it was in the National Council founded in 1903, rather than in Cumann na nGaedheal – the body to which he had first publicly outlined an alternative to armed revolution – that Griffith was to find more influential supporters.[41]

The publication of *The Resurrection of Hungary* was a momentous event in Irish history, although our contemporary term 'an instant hit' would be a misnomer for it. First, it appeared in serialised form from 2 January 1904 to 2 July 1904 in *The United Irishman*.[42] It aroused uncommon interest. A week later, on 9 July, Griffith wrote: 'last week we printed the conclusion of the articles on the *Resurrection of Hungary* and we have since received scores of letters urging that they should be republished in pamphlet form.'

In the format of a book, Griffith's work would merit the epithet of bestseller. It is, of course, a blueprint for gaining Irish independence, using the Hungarian method. The book is only 99 pages long, and consisting of an appendix, a set of mottoes, a preamble and twenty-seven short chapters, each packed with condensed information and cogent argument; yet the style is flowing and there is space for anecdote and reflection. It has been praised as one of the best Irish political pamphlets;[43] in our opinion there aren't many of this quality in any political literature.

The short 'Preamble' tells the reader that the alternative to armed resistance is not an acquiescence in tyranny but – a masterstroke of a delayed explosion –

39 *United Irishman*, 1 Nov. 1902.   **40** Ibid., 8 Nov. 1902.   **41** Cf. Hubert Mahony, 'Arthur Griffith and Cumann na nGaedheal', incompleted MA thesis, 1968 (photocopy in Griffith Archives, Russell Library, Maynooth College).   **42** Padraig Colum, 'Arthur Griffith' (typescript version, National Library Ms. 10,236), p. 160 notes the curious coincidence of *Resurrection's* appearance and the date 16 June 1904, of Leopold Bloom's perambulations in Dublin. The prototype of Joyce's Ulysses was a Dublin Jew of Hungarian origin. It is well known that some of Bloom's dreams and phantasies refer to Griffith's works. It is our conjecture that *The Resurrection* as a pamphlet was rediscovered in Hungary only through the first translation of Ulysses in 1947. Since that date the National Library acquired the 1918 edition of *The Resurrection* and some libraries and individuals also possess a copy of the 1904 or 1918 text.   **43** This success story has been described in varying detail by several authors but, perhaps, most accurately and pungently by Seán Ó Luing. While acknowledging his work as a source, it also helped in our own analysis of Griffith's thesis. Seán Ó Luing, *Art Ó Griofa* (Átha Cliath, 1953). Hereby we also acknowledge the help given by James Foran with the reading of texts in the Irish language.

the Hungarian parallel. What follows is a point by point analysis of the comparisons and lessons Griffith drew from juxtaposing events of Irish and Hungarian history; these reflect both Griffith's view of history and his method of placing emphasis on events of his choice; they may or may not be historically accurate. (The roman numerals indicate Griffith's chapter headings.)

I   Hungarians are introduced as brave, intelligent, prosperous; Hungary as intellectually outstanding, industrially or commercially significant. (Whatever the veracity of these statements, contemporary descriptions of Hungary by foreigners reflect this picture.) Yet – *Comparison 1* – Hungary in 1849 seemed as crushed as Ireland was in 1798. The potted history of Hungary that follows, from the conquest to loss of independence in 1526,[44] is as straightforward as any Magyar would wish it to be.[45]

II   The new era: Hungary had rid itself of one master (the Turk); she had found another (the Austrians). *Comparison 2* – Hungarian nobles became as thoroughly Germanicised as the Irish landlords were Anglicised. *Comparison 3* – Out of fear of the French Revolution Austria yielded in 1790 first as out of fear of the Volunteers England yielded to Ireland in 1782.

III   Hungary, 1794: Martinovics, conspiring for armed revolt, was crushed.[46] *Comparison 4* – (tyrants' tactics) Austria send Magyars to Italy, Italians to Hungary; Dublin fusiliers were sent to cut the throats of Boers.

IV   Széchenyi – the story of the ascendancy of the Hungarian language in the nineteenth century. In this section there are no parallels recalling the past; instead, there is a message loud and clear, which Griffith attributes to Széchenyi: revive your language, educate yourselves, build up your agriculture and your industries.[47] This was a call – the first shoot out of which the plant of Sinn Fein was to grow and burgeon.

V   Kossuth and Deák, the violent and non-violent approach. *Comparison 5* – Kossuth was as hearty a hater of Austria as John Mitchel[48] was of

44 Arminius Vámbéry, *Hungary* (5th edition, London, 1893); there is a copy in UCD library acquired at the turn of the century (no record of exact year of acquisition). This book, a typical account of Hungary's history in the Ausgleich era emphasises national concerns later depicted by Griffith. 45 Cf. A.J. Patterson, *The Magyars* (London, 1869), 2 vols. Griffith would have consulted the National Library copy, call no. 914. 39, p. 4. 46 Cf. L Leger, *History of Austria-Hungary* (London, 1889). National Library call no. 9436. Ll. 47 István Széchenyi (1791-1860) indeed has said all these things, but never succinctly, for he had a turgid style. Griffith might have consulted: John Paget, *Hungary and Transylvania* (2nd ed., London, 1850) and indeed, some of the count's own works in German, e.g. István Széchenyi, *Über dem Credit* (Vienna, 1830). 48 Although Griffith edited the *Jail journal* (John Mitchel, *Jail journal*, ed. with a preface and notes by Arthur Griffith,

England. *Comparison 6* – Deák took his stand on the Pragmatic Sanction[49] just 'as we in Ireland took our stand on the Settlement of 1782' (p. 17). In the rest of the chapter the early parliamentary career of the two leaders is sketched. Only one of Griffith's statements on Kossuth is inaccurate: 'His ambition was to see Hungary as an independent republic.' This contribution cannot be predated into the 1830s, because even when he dethroned the Habsburgs in April 1849 Kossuth kept the notion of a *Hungarian kingdom* intact. He was finally converted to being a republican in his captivity in Turkey in 1850.

VI   The *Pesth Gazette*[l] – Kossuth's newspaper – is described, with its great influence on public opinion, its total commitment to reform, and the institution it promoted: the Hungarian League of Industry and Commerce. No comparison is drawn but Griffith, again, points to a NEWSPAPER THAT COULD CHANGE PUBLIC OPINION (*Pesth Gazette – United Irishman*), secondly an ASSOCIATION – *Hungary by itself*, as it were – that was comprised of COUNTY COUNCILS. (Hungarian County Councils = actual depositories of local power; Irish Councils to be that.) Two further points of interest in this section: Hungary's 1848 revolution is presented as Kossuth's. No one can really quarrel with that, although it is an oversimplification. Griffith refers to M. Jókai, his favoured Hungarian novelist, whose stories he devoured in the National Library. '*Sons of the Baron* which deals with the Revolution of 1848 is invaluable in this respect.'[51] When we consider Griffith's statement: 'There is no book in English which gives anything like a detailed account of the Resurrection of Hungary' and

Dublin, 1914), his articles on the turn of the century show constant reading of Mitchel.   **49** *The Pragmatic Sanction* in 1723 was a constitutional provision to enable the female line of the Habsburgs – as well as the male line – to succeed to the Hungarian throne; cf. C.M. Knatchbull-Hugessen, *The political evolution of the Hungarian nation* (London, 1908), vol. 1, pp. 190-5. **50** The *Pesth gazette* = *Pesti Hirlap* is even more authentically described by Griffith than in the text he could have found in the likeliest source: P.C. Headley, *The authentic life of Louis Kossuth* (London, 1851). National Library call no. J92. He might well have consulted the *Pesti Hirlap* chapter in E.O.S., *Hungary and its revolutions* (London, 1854), pp. 222-5. (E.O.S. has recently been identified as Susan Horner.)   **51** In the 9 July issue of the *United Irishman* Griffith gave a short and incomplete summary of his reading: 'The life of Deák by M.E. Duffy; the memoirs of Kossuth, Klapka, Görgei and Count Beust; ... lives of Maria Theresa and Joseph II; Baron de Worms: Count Beust and the Settlement of Hungary; addresses of the Hungarian Diet of 1861 ... Boner's Transylvania, Patterson's the Magyars ... Jókai's novels ... Stiles History of the Revolutionary movements in Austria-Hungary ... statements by French, Italian, English statesmen 1848-1867, Leger's Austria-Hungary, ... histories of Austria and Prussia ..., Buda-Pesth newspapers, 1848-1867, ... The Times, 1848-49; 1861-5-6-7, ... several in the National Library, Emile Reclus supplies statistics on Austria-Hungary and official statistics from their embassies.' We also know from Griffith that he had been receiving material from

contrast it with his sources (or indeed anything that he might have read, but not listed, such as the book of Francis Pulszky and his wife Theresa),[52] we have to conclude that, although Griffith represented facts and views of the Hungarian 1848 tradition, no one had put those forward in the unique combination he did.

VII   The outbreak. The story of the Hungarian defence of their hard-won liberty, *with two lessons*: the oppressors revoke the constitution when it suits them; Hungary would not have fought without Kossuth's organising.

VIII   The Republic. In this section we meet Deák again making a peace move and failing; we encounter General Guyon[53] – of Irish stock – who fought decisive battles for Hungarian liberty; and we meet Kossuth in April 1849 as dictator of Hungary. (The mistake of believing that Hungary in 1848 became a republic is not unique to Griffith. One of his authorities, Stiles,[54] spoke in the same terms.)

IX   The treason of Görgei.[55] Griffith's authorities were divided on this question and he did not charge Görgei too harshly. In a desperate and totally hopeless situation in August 1849 General Arthur Görgei, 'the traitor', surrendered to the Russians. General George Klapka,[56] on the other hand, managed to settle terms for the surrender of his garrison and was called a hero. After that comes the iron rule of the Austrian general Haynau – *Comparison 7* – a replica of the British General Lake.[57]

X   The entombment. The chapter starts with an odious *example*. Austria was trying to excite religious animosity between Hungarian Catholics and Protestants. Then, *Comparison 8* in relation to the Austrian revenge: 'Count Louis Batthyány[58] the premier ... like Wolfe Tone ...

the Austro-Hungarian embassy. It is conjectured that he might have read the *Pester Lloyd* in the RDS but I have no proof of that. Alas, the RDS have dispersed their holdings since, some was given to NLI, some to diverse other libraries. My informant was Professor T.W. Moody, the first person I consulted on Griffith.   **52** The most popular being Ferenc Pulszky, *Mein Leben und Zeit* (Budapest, 1884); Theresa Pulszky, Memoirs of a *Hungarian lady* (London, 1850); Ferenc and Theresa Pulszky, *Tales and traditions of Hungary* (London, 1851), 2 vols.   **53** Richard Guyon (1812–56) was a Hungarian general of Anglo-Irish origin who fought in the war of liberation of 1849.   **54** W.H. Stiles, *Austria in 1848-1949* (New York, 1852), 2 vols.   **55** Arthur Görgey, *My life and acts in Hungary* (London, 1852), National Library call no. 94391 G1. (This was acquired before 1880 – no exact date available.)   **56** György Klapka, *Memoirs of the War of Independence in Hungary* (London, 1850), 2 vols.   **57** General Gerard Lake (1744-1808) ... 'engaged in disarming the population and counteracting the plans of the United Irishmen' (*DNB*, vol. 31, pp. 411-4). General Haynau was military overlord in conquered Hungary in 1849.   **58** Lajos Batthyány (1806-49), first prime minister of independent Hungary in 1848 was executed by the Austrians.

cheated the tyrants by cutting his throat' (p. 34). In exile some
Hungarian leaders decided to fight for Turkey – *Comparison 9* – so did
an Irishman, the Young Irelander Eugene O'Reilly ...

XI   The migration of Deák. Deák sold his estate in the country, moved to
the capital and started work to reclaim the Constitution. Deák wanted
the Constitution back – Repeal the Union – 'but Ireland had no Deák'
(p. 37), commented Griffith. Deák was faced with Bach[59] – *Comparison
10* – the Austrian Joseph Chamberlain,[60] but refused to deal with him
while the Hungarian Constitution was suspended. He urged passive
resistance.

XII   How Francis Joseph[61] visited Pesth. The chapter starts with *Comparison
11*: an Austrian garrison watched over Hungary, politely called a police
force 'even as the Royal Irish Constabulary is' (p. 39). And, just as 'even
an animosity and distrust are sought and kindled and kept alive between
Irish Catholic and Irish Protestant by the English government' – *Comparison 12* – so the Austrian government sought to kindle and keep alive
race-hatred in Hungary. The emperor's visit in 1857 was a fiasco.

XIII   The fall of Bach. Griffith's account of Kossuth's exile diplomacy and
the 1859 French-Italian campaign against Austria sums up masterfully
Kossuth's own narrative of these events.[62] Bach, a hardliner, was fired,
but Deák refused any deal with the emperor and bided his time for the
parliament of 1861.

XIV   How the Hungarians refused to send representatives to the imperial
parliament. The emperor's new chancellor von Schmerling attempted to
placate the Hungarians with a local parliament that delegated deputies
to Vienna. *Comparison 13* – 'Forty years later certain English statesmen
have rediscovered Schmerling's[63] proposed policy and labelled it *Home
rule*' (p. 48). *Lesson* (Griffith's trump-card) Deák stays firm on the laws
of 1848 and states in the Hungarian parliament (Griffith's capitals):
'WE CANNOT RECOGNISE THE RIGHT OF THE SAID IMPERIAL
PARLIAMENT TO LEGISLATE ON THE AFFAIRS OF HUNGARY'
(p. 50).

XV   And how the emperor of Austria lost his temper. An account of the
dialogue between the king (his ministers) and Deák (the Diet). Griffith
summarises the process of negotiations.

59 Alexander Bach (1813-93), Austrian minister of Home Affairs in the early 1850's. **60** Joseph
Chamberlain (1836-1914), British statesman. **61** Francis Joseph (1830-1916), emperor of Austria,
king of Hungary. **62** Lajos Kossuth, *Memoirs of my exile* (London, 1880), National Library call
no. 9439 K4. **63** Anton Von Schmerling (1805-97) Austrian Minister of State.

XVI   The bloodless war – concerning exchanges in the press. *Lesson*: 'Fortunately for England, Ireland has never resorted to passive resistance' (p. 57). Griffith implies that an Irish press campaign would help the cause of Ireland.

XVII   The failure of force and conciliation. *Lesson*: 'Hungarian deputies continued to meet, not indeed as the Parliament of Hungary, but as the Hungarian Agriculture Union, the Hungarian Industrial League, etc.' (p. 58). Deák declares the Hungarian nation will never give up the Constitution.[64]

XVIII   The royal visit of 1865 – the emperor's dialogue continues with Deák.

XIX   Austria's last dodge. In 1865 the emperor calls the Hungarian parliament and awaits its submission but – *lesson* – unlike Ireland, Hungary, having learned not to trust the Austrians (p. 64) and aborted the meeting of the Hungarian Diet of 1865. Had the people – negative comparison, positive lesson – been Irish ... the emperor would have been declared the greatest man ... ; as for the Hungarians, they only said: 'Francis Joseph is a trickster' (p. 65). In other words the Hungarians rejected the emperor's new proposals. And thereby Griffith puts in *Comparison 15* – 'Mr Gladstone's second Home Rule Bill (1893) was modelled on this Austrian proposal.' Bismarck,[65] satisfied that Hungary would not rally to Austria's aid, declared war on her in June 1866.

XXI   The Austrian-Prussian war of 1866 – Austria was defeated; the emperor turned to Deák for advice. 'Make peace and restore Hungary to her rights' (an historical fact, but Griffith presents it as another lesson to be learnt). *Comparison 16* – almost as important to resist the demands of Hungary in 1866 as England was to resist the demands of Ireland in 1792, when, returning beaten from America, she found herself confronted in Ireland by 200,000 armed ... men' (p. 68).

XXII   Count Beust[66] – the new chancellor – advised the emperor to accede to the demands of the Deák party.

XXIII   The surrender of Austria. Hungary's constitution restored the narrative of Hungary's triumph. But wait for the punchline, which is a

---

64 Cfr. *Addresses of the Hungarian Diet* (London, 1861). See also its report in the *Freeman's Journal*, 28 August 1861.   65 Prince Otto von Bismarck (1815-98), German chancellor, victor of the 1866 Prussian-Austrian war.   66 Count Friedrich Ferdinand Beust (1809-86) statesman of Saxon origin, became the Austrian Foreign Secretary in 1866 and, with Deák, the architect of the *Compromise*. In English translation his memoir was one of Griffith's significant sources: *Aus drei Viertel-Jahrhunderten* (Stuttgart, 1887), 2 vols. = *Memoirs of Count Friedrich Ferdinand Beust* (London, 1887).

GIANT LESSON: 'Hungary who won her independence by refusing to send members to the Imperial Parliament ... has prospered ... ; we have to convince some very practical people that the fight for Ireland's independence, if present circumstances do not permit it to be waged with sword and gun, is nevertheless not the alternative to be fought out on the floor of the British House of Commons' (p. 73).

XXIV   The Ausgleich.[67] Griffith sets out the terms precisely, his summary is fair: Austria agreed to uphold the independence of Hungary and the full power of her parliament; Hungary retained her national army, ensigns, language, legal system; there were separate ministries except for 'three common factors': foreign, defence, finance. Francis Joseph was crowned king. Deák declined the office of prime minister.[68] Griffith dwelt on this aspect of the Hungarian saga repeatedly; he was presumably finding in Deák's modesty a personal lesson for the future.

XXV   Present and past Hungary. Using statistical data, Griffith, in a brilliant essay, outlined the economic progress of Hungary between 1867 and 1903. What he said cannot be faulted, but by being silent on certain things he painted a rosier picture than some contemporary social analysts. His statistics of an 18-million-strong Hungary enjoying an economic boom was not a false one, and it reflected his sources, but he was silent about the abject poverty of the over three million agrarian labourers of Hungary.[69] Ireland had had a land reform initiated by Gladstone, but Hungary – this negative comparison would have favoured Ireland – had none, until late 1918. But apart from *parliamentary debates* in Hungarian, such information on this aspect of life was practically inaccessible for a non-Hungarian. Griffith's authorities – such as R.G. Patteson, whom quoted twice in this section – were overstating even the cultural impact of Reform in post-Compromise Hungary, saying that in 1820 there was no national museum, no

67 Ausgleich = Compromise = Kiegyezés (Hungarian).   68 The description follows the memoirs of Beust and that of Deák – Ferenc Deák, *A Hungarian statesman. A memoir* (London, 1880), ational Library call no. 4939 D1. As we have seen, Griffith read the novels of Jókai for their historical social and literary content. Alas, the novels of Kálmán Mikszáth, the poems of Endre Ady (all locked in the Hungarian tongue) were inaccessible to him. These depicted how, together with genuine achievements, feudal privileges were also rescued, preserved. Hungary had no equivalent to the Church Disestablishment Act or to the Land Act of 1880. Nor could Griffith consult the Croatian, Czech or Romanian critics of the Compromise, who said in their mother tongues that the two strongest nations had agreed to rule over the weaker ones. They found an advocate to their cause in Seton Watson, who, under the pseudonym of Scotus Viator, wrote a series of pro-Slav, anti-Magyar articles in the early 1900s. His most influential book, published in London in 1907, was entitled *The future of Austria-Hungary*, appearing between the 2nd and 3rd edition of the *Resurrection*.

academy, no capital, implying that the language revival was sudden and that the National Theatre and National University had just sprung up – thus Griffith could draw his *negative comparison-lesson* saying that if only Ireland could concentrate on native culture it would soon have everything that Hungary can be proud of.[70] Now for the *Comparison 17*: 'Hungarian Michaels' had been to the Austrians figures of fun, as Irish Paddies still were to the English. *18*: The Hungarians had been called 'slovenly and unclean,' the Irish were still called 'dirty Irish'. *19*: They had called the Hungarians barbarous and ignorant which was what the English still called the Irish.

XXVI and XXVII   (These two chapters formed as one in the first edition.) Hungary and Ireland. *Comparison 20* – providing Griffith with a brilliant analysis – was in fact put forward in 1865 by one of his sources, the Englishman Charles Boner:[71] 'A Hungarian always dwells on his wrongs ... and, like the Irish, never loses an opportunity of putting them forward prominently' (p. 82). Boner found similarity in the Hungarian and Irish character, chided the Magyars for reviving their language and for wanting to share their own parliament, and perceived that 'Hungary for the Hungarians' was the same rallying cry as 'Ireland for the Irish.' (p. 85). At the time as Hungary produced the resilient Deák – Griffith laments – Ireland produced Isaac Butt,[72] who led the country to destruction.

The rest of the chapter is basically a set of points highlighting how the illegality of Ireland being governed by the British parliament had originated. Griffith made the following points:

(a)   Irish parliaments prior to the end of the eighteenth century had little real power, but the genius of Swift united most of Ireland against England.
(b)   The American war of Independence placed the game in Ireland's hand, the Irish volunteers gave a lead on the 'Non-importation Agreement' and displayed religious tolerance, and 300 Irish Protestants resolved in the

---

70 Tibor Klaniczay, *A history of Hungarian literature* (Budapest, 1982) and Hóman-Szekfü, op. cit. vol. 5, are two of the many authorities whose work refer to the beginnings of these cultural achievements. Thus in 1820 there were Hungarian theatres, albeit not a national one; Buda-Pest was already *de facto* the capital, although not *de jure*; the prototype of the Academy was already in existence; the collections that formed the national library cum museum had been donated to the nation in 1802, and the language of the country was predominantly Magyar although the burghers of Pest spoke mainly German and the aristocrats spoke mainly German or French.   **71** Charles Boner, *Transylvania: its products and people* (London, 1865). Griffith used the National Library copy call no. 914392 B9.   **72** Isaac Butt, 'father of Home Rule' (1813-79), was heavily criticised by Griffith.

church of Dungannon 'to make laws to bind this kingdom' (p. 88). Force was met by the required measure: the Renunciation Act by England was a reaction to the Irish Volunteers force, 200,000 men strong.

(c)   Unconsciously Grattan[73] was used by the English government in disband- ing the Volunteers. Yet, although it went into abeyance, 'the Parliament of Ireland has as legal an existence as it had in the year 1783' (p. 89). In the previous chapters Griffith built an intelligent edifice of twenty authentic *comparisons*, a host of *lessons* and several pointed *examples* into a network which, when reaching the twenty-fifth chapter, the reader must see to be a *valid parallel*. Henceforth any comparison, whether repeated or drawn afresh, would roll smoothly and swiftly on real parallel lines. Thus: 'we are in Ireland in regard to the settlement of 1783, precisely in the position of Hungary in regard to the Constitution of 1848' (p. 89).

(d)   All the 'constitutional' leaders who followed Grattan 'from O'Connell to Parnell worked on the assumption that the Act of Union was binding' (p. 90). To Griffith it was clearly illegal. Example: Beust criticised Gladstone's Home Rule Bill because it had not set up an independent parliament for Ireland. He explained (*lesson*) that Austria was forced to consent to the Hungarian demands because of the passive resistance Hungary had been displaying. Beust argued that, unlike Hungary, Ireland (a weakness in her claim) had not a separate language and literature and she had '*given her case away by sending members to the British Parliament*' (p. 91, Griffith's italics). Griffith countered these arguments: Ireland did have her own language and literature, and groups such as the United Irishmen did oppose parliamen- tary representation in Britain. He claimed that the five beneficial measures passed by the Westminister parliament – the Catholic Emancipation Act, the Tithes Act, the Church Disestablishment Act, the Land Act of 1881, the Local Government Act – 'were passed as a result of the unconscious carrying out by the people of the Hungarian policy' (p. 91, Griffith's italics). *Comparison – Lesson*: 'We must retrace our steps and take our stand on the Constitution of 1782 and the Renunciation Act, as Deák took his ... on the Laws of 1848' (p. 92).

(e)   The attempt of the Council of Three Hundred – which never met – should be revived as 'the initial step for Ireland to take in the application of what we have styled the 'Hungarian policy'' (p. 90).

(f)   As in (e) here Griffith builds on his earlier *examples* and *lessons* in formu- lating 'certain details of the new Hungarian policy: 'Five-sixths of Ireland would be represented in the Council ... as five-sixths of Hungary was represented ... in the "Agricultural Union"'' (p. 73).

[73] Henry Grattan (1746-1820), statesman and orator, came under strong criticism from Griffith.

(g)   Example – The County Councils of Hungary constituted the strongest
        weapon of national self-expression for Kossuth ... 'and Deák ... the County
        Councils of Ireland possess in some respects greater powers ...' (p. 94). The
        annual sum of £25,000 is raised annually for the upkeep of an important
        Irish parliamentary party in the British parliament. This sum could help
        Irish trade.

(h)   A system of protection for Irish manufacturers – *example* – like the Hun-
        garian Védegylet Association[74] should be set up.

(i)   Local Arbitration Courts should be established.

(j)   The summing of the parallel and the policy: where matters of Hungary
        differ from those of Ireland, Irishmen can adapt the details to their own
        needs; '*what the Hungarians did for Hungary Irishmen can do for Ireland*' (p.
        96, my italics).

Griffith's argument is followed by three appendices: a note on the novels and the
achievements of Maurus Jókai,[75] a reproduction of the Renunciation Act, and a
set of comparative statistics for 1871 and 1904 which show a decline in
population and in land under tillage in Ireland but an increase in taxation and
pauperism.

All in all: by championing the Hungarian cause, by reflecting what Hungary,
through its national historians and benevolent foreign observers wished to
project, Griffith built up an authentic, if over-optimistic,[76] picture of a country
in East Central Europe – a picture Hungarians liked to see when looking into the
mirror of their own history but, because it was an optimal representation of
available facts, one they could never fully draw for themselves. And as for its
wider implications we accept Justice Lennon's judgement: 'It is doubtful if, in
the history of political pamphlets in Ireland, there has been any other which
produced, eventually, such far reaching results.'[77] No doubt he did make political
use of history, but writing political history is, *ab ovo*, a selection of events and
views that reflect the historical period depicted in a certain contemporary light.
Griffith's summaries depicted the main issues also centrally portrayed by

74 Védegylet (Hungarian Protective Association) was promoted by Kossuth in the mid-1840s for
the protection of Hungarian manufacture. It was not nearly as successful in economic as in political
terms (cf. Hóman-Szekfü, op. cit., vol. 5, ch. 3), which Griffith might not have known as the
Kossuth literature accessible to him described it as an unqualified success.   75 Mór Jókai (1825-
1904) was perhaps the greatest; or at least the most popular Hungarian novelist. From the list of his
novels given by Griffith the following are still extant in the National Library: *Debts of Honour* (1900),
call no. 894411 J3; *Hungarian sketches in peace and war* (1855), call no. T894411; *The Green Book of
Freedom under the Snow* (1897), call no. 894411 J2; *Midst the wild Carpathians* (1897), call no. 894411
Jl. These were all in the N.L. during Griffith's day.   76 Not even the most optimistic of
contemporary Hungarian historians, Henrik Marczali, *Übersicht der Geschichte Ungarns* (Budapest,
1918) was as complimentary as Griffith, but he made the same points.   77 Lennon, op. cit., p.127.

contemporary historians. In terms of Hungarian history they were vital issues, in terms of Irish events: decisive ones. It should be noted that subsequent editions of the *Resurrection* were classified by the Library of the British Museum as 'Hungarian history – appendix' which shows that they had taken the historical authenticity of the work seriously.

Of the reactions to the work one of the first and most seminal, Tom Kettle's, has been deservedly noted by Griffith's biographers (Ó Luing, Lennon). He publicly posed the question: 'Would the Hungarian policy work?'[78] Similar questions – as can be seen in their correspondence – were posed by Alice Milligan and Terence McSwiney. The new Sinn Fein, arising out of 'the Hungarian policy', ought, in McSwiney's opinion, to take as its starting point Wolfe Tone's declaration of faith from the dock: 'he had seen the connection between Great Britain and Ireland to be a source of Ireland's misfortunes and accordingly he strove to sever the connection'.[79] McSwiney thought that Griffith, in the *United Irishman*, ought to lend its pages to the expression of separation. Between March and July 1905,[80] therefore, Griffith published a series of articles on the 'working of the policy – a short sequel to the Resurrection of Hungary'.[81] Griffith returned to the subject of the 1782 Constitution's legality and the Council of Three Hundred (ideas to be marked out as transferred into the politics of the day), the point about American financial aid, a levy to raise revenue for the proposed Council, a basis of a competent national civil service. Griffith stressed how, in the period of passive resistance, non-cooperating Hungarian civil servants paralysed the administration. He enlarged upon the idea of national arbitration courts, the question of industrial enterprise and liquid capital. He said that Kossuth had shown that the support of the Hungarian County Councils – who had chosen to pool their money – enabled the setting up and successful functioning of the Hungarian National Bank. In terms of foreign

78 *New Ireland Review*, February 1905.   79 Terence McSwiney to Alice Milligan, 25 Mar., 7 Dec. 1905, copies (NLI Ms. 1649).   80 Before the March series Griffith published in the 21 January issue of the *United Irishman* an excerpt from the *Pesth Gazette* of 1843 and wrote: 'Our situation is that of a man in prison. If England will give us neither legal protection for our industries, nor regulate her commercial relations with us by the laws of justice and equality, Ireland must endeavour by social means, by the free will of her people to secure that protection for her struggling industries which is refused by law. Like England herself, who at one time rejected the silk and woollen manufactures of the East Indies and was content with her own inferior goods for the sake of promoting her domestic industry – like America, whose sons at first depended on English wares to supply the want of home manufacturers, but later prided themselves on being worse clothed that they might learn to make better stuffs – so most patriotic Irishwomen voluntarily determined for a period, to use nothing but the manufactures of Ireland even if inferior – since the nation can only thus be indemnified for the compulsion to which it must yield, and by forcing the foreigners out of the markets, revive the national prosperity' (communicated by Professor Richard Davies, University of Tasmania).   81 *United Irishman* 18 March – 10 June 1905.

policy Irish troops must be withdrawn from South Africa, and all in all, the whole present machinery could be choked, *without violence, by passive resistance*[82] (my italics).

By the end of the year D.P. Moran's *Leader* was to call Sinn Féin scornfully the 'Green Hungarian band'. Griffith's friends in the newly formed Sinn Féin accepted the proposed Hungarian policy. In his introduction to the first-ever pamphlet of Sinn Féin, Griffith wrote: "(I) urged that the policy of Hungary pursued in its contact with Austria (1849-1867) was in essence the policy of national dignity and political wisdom directed to be followed by Ireland' (p. 2).[91]

Griffith, of course, would have been the last to be doctrinaire about this policy. In this same year the *United Irishman* ceased publication and was replaced by the weekly entitled *Sinn Fein*. In its pages Griffith explored the work of Friedrich List,[83] the apostle of protectionism, and how List's teaching was successfully applied in Germany. In choosing the German example Griffith must have gathered that Hungary – which advocated the Listian approach in 1847 – had later deviated from the path of strict protectionism. When recommending it to Ireland, Griffith could not have considered that the economic dynamism of large countries, rich in resources, were fundamentally different from that of small countries. When discussing protectionism, Griffith drew on the example of Germany and talked also of other countries *such as* Hungary and Poland. Of course, Hungary was his primary example, Hungary of 1904, a large country, a viable economic unit with considerable industry and agriculture by that time. Thus his economic argument, running through many pamphlets and many years between 1907 and 1915, is less valid than his political one.[84]

But at Easter 1916 something happened which – to say the least – placed a question mark against the Deák-Griffith way of non-violent, passive resistance. Those involved in the Easter rising had had the same spiritual patrimony as Griffith himself; just as Kossuth had had the same patrimony as Deák; moreover, the insurgents had all benefited from Griffith's writing and political activities, yet they chose the alternative he wished to avoid. Griffith's biographers repeatedly stressed that,

---

82 *Ibid.*, 22 July 1905; in 1908 Griffith, in a letter to the 'Men of Leitrim' (as quoted by Lennon, *op. cit.*, p. 132) argued that the idea of parliamentary non-cooperation had a precedent in J.D. Trotter's attitude to tax: cf. Younger, op. cit., p. 27.   83 28 November 1905 under the presidency of Edward Martyn. Cf. Arthur Griffith, *The Sinn Féin policy* (Dublin, 1906). There is a letter dated 'Monday' (1906?) in the National Library from Griffith to Walter Cole, in which he requests 'the minute book of the Hungarian Committee.' This suggests that such a Committee existed and Cole was, probably its secretary. The existence of this letter was recorded by Hubert Mahony (who had copied it out) amongst the notes to his unfinished MA thesis. I could not relocate it in the NL. There were of course those who rejected outright the Dual Monarchy concept within that policy – for example, *Irish Freedom* (April and October 1911), under the editorship of Bulmer Hobson.   84 Friedrich List, *The national system of political economy* (London, 1840).

although Griffith had admired Deák immensely, he denied that he could ever be the 'Irish Deák',[85] a role he thought should have been filled by Grattan in his own time.

For the purposes of our study we have to be content with a restatement of the 'Hungarian policy' as it was reflected in the pamphlet *Ireland Looks into the Mirror* and in the augmented version of *The Resurrection of Hungary*. The author of the pamphlet, who identified himself only as D,[86] re-stated the case of non-violent approach, writing at the time when, in the wake of the Easter rising, most nationalist leaders, including Griffith, were in jail. On twelve pages the pamphlet summarised the arguments of *The Resurrection* and referred to arguments in *Griffith's Sinn Féin Policy*, a pamphlet that translated the theoretical parallels into points of actual policy. In the opening paragraph of the pamphlet Griffith extended the framework and claimed that within the British Empire 'Bengal had adopted the same policy' of self-reliance and passive resistance. In the penultimate section of the pamphlet (p. 27) he referred to the success of the National Bank of Hungary, established by Kossuth in 1842. The remaining sections of the pamphlet were points of a unified campaign – following Hungary's example – to promote in Ireland: a national university, industries, a national system of political economy, a National Council, protectionism, a merchant navy, an Irish consular service, a poor law system, a national civil service, national courts of law, an anti-enlistment movement, a strike against taxes, a national stock exchange and a banking system. In 1916 'D' took the view that this Sinn Féin policy was yet to be tried to the full. At the end of his pamphlet, after drawing up a comparative tabulation of Hungarian and Irish historical events, he stated: '1916 Irish Republic proclaimed. Insurrection crushed. Redmond and the "eighty seven party" accept partition proposals. Partition abandoned owing to Irish hostility 1917?'[87] We know from

85 Arthur Griffith, *How Ireland is taxed* (Dublin, 1917); *Economic salvation and the means to attain it* (Dublin, 1911); *When the government publishes sedition: the census report on Ireland and the annual finance return* (Dublin, 1915); *To rebuild a small nation* (Dublin, 1916). The economic 'evidence' for the last pamphlet was the British trade returns for 1914 which show Britain as Ireland's top trading partner. But Griffith's conclusions are questionable. Griffith's political pamphlets where the economic argument is not dominant: *Dublin Castle exhumed* (Dublin, 1916) and *Small nations* (Dublin, 1917), grew out of articles in his three newspapers, the *United Irishman*, *Sinn Fein* and *nationality*, the last of which was started in 1915 with a new series in 1917. *Small nations* was released by the National Council of Sinn Féin. 86 Griffith wrote in the *United Irishman*, 23 July 1904, 'The Irish Deák must be a man who can accept an Ireland united with England just so far as Hungary is united with Austria ... Had the writer of these articles been a Hungarian he would have been a supporter of Kossuth and approved Kossuth's proclamation in 1849 (i.e. dethroning the Habsburgs) which Deák did not approve.' Other writers who noted Griffith's fondness of Deák were Seán Ó Luing, *Art Ó Griofa* (Baile Atha Cliath, 1953); Calton Younger, *Arthur Griffith* (Dublin, 1981); Richard P. Davis, *Arthur Griffith and the non violent Sinn Fein* (Dublin, 1974); Virginia E. Gladston, *Arthur Griffith and the advanced nationalism from Ireland 1900-1922* (New York, 1905); Padraic Colum, *Arthur Griffith* (Dublin, 1959). 87 'D'. could not be identified with any certainty. It could not be John Dillon as 'Dillonism' is attacked in the pamphlet, nor Joseph Devlin or George Gavan

many sources that when the pamphlet was issued Griffith was in Reading gaol and practising passive resistance towards his captors.

The extended argument by Sinn Féin was used again in 1917 in the pamphlet entitled *Small Nations*[88] in which Ireland was grouped with Poland, Hungary, Greece and others, and that the National Council of Sinn Féin uses the same argument as Griffith was to re-state in the (third) 1918 edition of the *Resurrection*. In other words Griffith, with some silent forces of the non-violent Sinn Féin still pleading the case, once more pointed towards the peaceful way of a wider European application which, via the example of smaller nations, should also be appropriate for Ireland.

The comparison between the 1904 and the 1918 texts reveals a 6 per cent change of the original text but a 60 per cent increase of the 1918 edition.[89] I speak of *texts* instead of editions, because the '1st' edition was in journal form, the '2nd' edition was virtually the same as the first in pamphlet form, the '3rd' was the 1918 augmented edition. But these various editions were never systematically described as 1st, 2nd and 3rd. Often the '2nd' edition is called '1st' and the '3rd' edition '2nd'. Hence my use of the terms '1904 text' and the '1918 text'. The 2nd edition, that is, the first book format, ran to 99 pages; the 3rd edition to 168 pages. Because of the differences in layout, the two are not exactly comparable. It is fair to say that the '1918 text' had a percentage increase of 60 over the '1904 text', the increase occurring mainly in the 1918 text's preface, introduction and appendices.[90]

Continuing to read widely about Hungary, Griffith has certainly absorbed information presented by two authors on Hungary: Knatchbull-Hugessen[91] and Arthur Delisle.[92] Most of the additions are an inclusion of a series of 17 articles on 'Pitt's policy', reprinted from 1911, as well as the *Sinn Féin policy* and an article on 'The economic oppression of Ireland'. The 1918 text is in fact Griffith's own mature presentation of his policy. The most significant of the alterations refer to republicanism, which is no longer seen as the *sine qua non* by Griffith. He seems to have understood from his new reading and from the events of history (although Francis Joseph died in 1916, the Hungarians did not declare a republic) that even Kossuth was no republican[93] until he was forced into exile; and he was increasingly

---

Duffy for they were not the closest supporters of Griffith. Printed by Whelan and Son, in 1916, the pamphlet was issued as 'Tracts for Irishmen, No. 1.' (Copy in RIA) Ibid. p. 27.   88 'D', op. cit., p. 14.   89 National Council of Sinn Féin, *Small Nations* (Dublin, August 1917).   90 Arthur Griffith, *The resurrection of Hungary* (3rd ed., Dublin, 1918), compared with the 2nd ed. (Dublin, 1904).   91 Hubert Mahony went a long way analysing the difference in his unfinished ms. study of Griffith's work.   92 He would have read in the National Library: C.M. Knatchbull Hugessen, *The political evolution of the Hungarian nation* (London, 1908). It should be noted that this author based much of his thorough research on the best Hungarian authority of the reform period: Mihály Horváth, *Huszonöt év Magyarország történetéből* (Geneva, 1864).   93 Arthur Delisle, *Hungary ...* (London, 1914) is mentioned and quoted in the 1918 edition. Griffith must have owned a copy.

convinced that the composition of Irish society would hardly allow a ready transition of Catholics and Protestants into a United Republican Ireland.[94]

The second important change is a milder attitude noticeable in Griffith's treatment of Görgei's surrender in 1849. This might have been due to the weight of new argument.[95]

The third change involves the role of language in Hungary which (by 1918) was the only language of some millions whose fathers had spoken not a word of it. This was meant to indicate the success of the Hungarian language movement – a success somewhat exaggerated by Griffith in his efforts to promote the Irish language by way of example. What did happen between 1867 and 1914 was the official promotion of the Hungarian language to the detriment of minority ethnic languages in Hungary. Its forceful application would not have pleased Deák, who had said that every nationality had the right to facilities for the education of its children in its own language. Hungary of 1867 had a six million Magyar population (as by 'race') plus a ten million non-Magyar population = sixteen million; Hungary of 1914 had a ten million Magyar population (as by language) plus a nine million non-Magyar population = nineteen million. 'Racially' the Magyars made very little advance, but linguistically their progress had been immense. Four million more people claimed to be Magyars than c.50 years earlier. Where Griffith erred was that in 1867 even those who claimed to be non-Magyars, racially, may have spoken some Magyar. Indeed, many would have spoken Magyar as their second language. What really happened, therefore, was that in 1914 there were 4 million more people whose first language was Magyar than in 1867.[97] The last addition Griffith made was a list of Hungary's Sinn Féin institutions.

In summary we may unequivocally state that Arthur Griffith presented and represented a clear and authoritative document to the Irish nation drawn upon facts and views of Hungarian history as chronicled by Hungarian historians and foreign observers of Hungary. His mistakes were few, his argument was valid. Like all good politicans, he was standing on the shoulder of patriots, and thereby he established, in 1904, a new political position which was still recognised as valid in 1919: 'The political position we are in is due principally to the teaching of Arthur Griffith (declared a Sinn Féin meeting in the Mansion House on 31 May) and the greatest tribute that can be paid to a man is that what he thought yesterday Ireland is thinking today.'[98]

---

94 Lennon, op. cit., pp. 139-40 argues that Griffith modified his stand as a result of further reading. Nonetheless, the 1918 edition carries the portraits of the king and queen of Hungary as well as that of Deák.   95 'For Griffith, Irish Nationality was not based upon race or creed; it was based instead upon the indissoluble unity of the whole people of Ireland in one community': V.E. Glandon, *Arthur Griffith and the advanced-nationalist press* (New York, 1985), p. 42.   96 C.M. Knatchbull-Hugessen, op. cit., vol. 2, p. 81 quoted Arthur Görgey, *Mein Leben und Wirken in Ungarn* (Vienna, 1852) in which the commander justified the surrender.   97 Ferenc Deák, *Beszédei* (Budapest, 1872), p. 339. 98 Quoted by Lennon, op. cit., 10/1.

2

The Irish and the Hungarian 1848

Your Excellencies, ladies and gentlemen![1]

Eighteen forty-eight was one hundred and fifty years ago, yet in some sense it is still with us, alive not only as history, but as the real beginning of a process that led to the full independence of our two countries, Ireland and Hungary.

Indeed, every beginning builds on a previous beginning in history. Ireland in 1998 also celebrates the results of 1798 (a much larger-scale affair for the same goals) and Hungary had its own Jacobins, who were filled with the same spirit of freedom and who died martyrs' deaths in 1795.

Seventeen ninety-eight fuelled to the Young Irelanders, led by William Smith O'Brien; Jacobin notions were ammunition for Sándor Petöfi, and his circle, who sparked off the Hungarian Revolution of 1848.

O'Brien and his comrades were originally reformers. I have two pamphlets in my library written by O'Brien. One proposes Church reforms; the other, political innovation.

The year 1848 was preceded by a period of Hungarian history now called the 'reform era'. Practically all the *main* participants of 1848 (Kossuth, Széchenyi,

---

[1] An alphabetical list of suggestions for further reading:

István Deák, *The lawful revolution* (*The Hungarian 1848*) (New York, 1979)
Michel Doheny, *The felon's track*, ed. Arthur Griffith (Dublin, 1914)
E.O.S. (Susan Horner), *Hungary and its rRevolutions* (London, 1854)
Freeman's Journal, 20, 23, 24, 25 June 1864 (all on W.S. O'Brien)
Thomas Kabdebo, *Blackwall Küldetése* (Budapest, 1990)
Thomas Kabdebo, *Hungary and Ireland* (Maynooth, 1992)
John Mitchel, *Jail journal*, ed. Arthur Griffith (Dublin, 1921)
Thomas Moore, 'Forget not the field' translated by S. Petöfi, *Életképek*, 24 September 1848
William Smith O'Brien, *Thoughts upon ecclesiastical reform* (Limerick, 1833)
William Smith O'Brien, *Speech ... on the causes of discontent in Ireland* (Dublin, 1843)
William Smith O'Brien, Diaries ... diary for 1861. In Mss. (the property of Mr Anthony O'Brien);
Sándor Petöfi, *The poems of Alexander Petöfi*, translated by John Bowring (London, 1864).

Klauzál, Szemere, Batthyány, and others) were reformers and were seeking to lift the country economically as well as to liberate it on a gradual basis. Hungary had a parliament and, although it was firmly under the control of the Austrian government and king, reforms were trickling through.

Politically, the Irish had less freedom of movement. In the absence of an independent parliament, Irish MPs had to operate in Westminster. Although some individuals stood out as having achieved reform (the greatest being Daniel O'Connell, with Catholic emancipation) it was not until Parnell, that is to say much later, that Ireland could and did have a strong party in Westminster. When his turn came, Parnell fashioned his ideas to incorporate some of the aims of the Young Irelanders, but travelling on an evolutionary, not a revolutionary, road.

It must be observed that Britain's military power was much greater than that of Austria. Consequently the Irish were much more constrained and hemmed in in 1848 than were the Hungarians. O'Brien himself was an MP, greatly concerned with the aged and the helpless poor of Ireland, as well as with education and free emigration. In 1846 he was reappointed a Justice of the Peace in Limerick. He endeavoured to redress the grievances of the system of government. In July 1846 he seemed to have strengthened his ties with Duffy, Meagher and Mitchel and formed the Irish Confederation. Early in 1848 O'Brien proclaimed the United Irelander resolution to establish an Irish parliament.

The combined effects of the French revolution of 1848 and the pressure of the Irish famine, however, accelerated the course of events, and on 15 March 1848 O'Brien addressed a great meeting of the Confederates in the music hall in Abbey Street, Dublin, where he urged the formation of a national guard, and added that he had recently deprecated the proposal that the people ought to be trained in military expertise; but he said, circumstances were entirely altered, and he now thought that the attention of intelligent young men should be turned to such questions as how strong places could be captured and weak ones defended. Accompanied by Meagher and Holywood, O'Brien went to Paris to present a congratulatory address from the Confederation to the newly formed French Republic. They were received by Lamartine, whose refusal to interfere with the internal affairs of the British Empire was a great disappointment to the deputation, whose principal object had been to awaken sympathy for Ireland in France.

The government had now resolved to proceed against the leaders of the Confederation. O'Brien's incriminating speech was delivered on 15 March 1848; he was subsequently tried but was not convicted. On 29 March Mitchel was sentenced to transportation; Duffy, Martin and others were arrested.

Eighteen forty-eight was, as we know, a year of fermentation in Europe. Between January and mid-March, revolts and revolutions broke out in Milan, Paris, Munich, Vienna and Pest (or let us say Pest-Buda, as the Hungarian capital was then called). The Hungarian parliament was in session in the west of the country, debating reform, while Hungarian writers, in other words Young Hungary, were in conference in Pest in the Pilvax coffee house.

The poet Petöfi wrote a rousing poem, called the 'National Song', which he recited three times to growing crowds in Pest:

> The sword is brighter than the chain,
> And on the arm a nobler gain,
> Yet you would think chains were preferred!
> Come to our aid, ancestral sword.

If some of you recognised the direct influence of Thomas Moore's poetry on these four lines, you were not mistaken. Hungarians translated Moore profusely.

Moore, of course, was no revolutionary, but his words could ignite Hungarian revolutionary fire. Petöfi and his friends drafted a twelve-point programme, which was printed at a printing works taken over by the revolutionaries, who proceeded to open the doors of a political prison, linked up with the students of the university and – in the wake of a waning municipal authority – formed a Revolutionary Council. Within a week their programme was adopted by the parliament. Ferdinand, the king in Vienna, was advised to give his consent to the establishment of a free Hungarian government, whose only link to the Austrian court was the foreign ministry. Foreign affairs were supposed to be jointly dealt with by the Austrian and Hungarian foreign ministries. So far the revolution had been bloodless in the month of March, and the new laws were voted in and enacted in April.

Meanwhile in Ireland the Confederate leader had decided to bring about an insurrection, which he hoped would attract the united support of the landed gentry. On behalf of the British government the lord lieutenant, Clarendon, had Duffy, Martin and others arrested. O'Brien was trying to drum up support in the south. On his return, a war directory of five was appointed in Dublin: Dillon, Meagher, O'Gorman, McGee and Devin Reilly. Having toured the countryside enlisting support (but securing mainly peasants armed only with pikes), O'Brien attacked a body of police on Boulah Common. The police were better armed and the insurrection ended the same day it started, 29 July 1848.

At that time in Hungary and in Austria, special commissioners were appointed to deal with the 'bi-focal' revolution. The people of Pest and the people of Vienna – both led by their younger element – lynched the commissioners and obeyed only their own leaders. The Austrian court had secretly negotiated an invasion by the Croatian general Jellachich and he, with his Croatian army, started to move into the heart of Hungary. The Hungarian prime minister, Batthyány, negotiated with Jellachich in vain. The radical politician Kossuth took over the leadership, declared war on the Croats and the newly formed Hungarian army chased them out of the country. These events take us to the end of September 1848.

Britain, too, was affected by the events of 1848, partly through parliament and its radicals, and partly through the Chartists, the most left-wing of all British political conglomerations to date. Yet there was no danger of the type of instability they greatly feared in Ireland. O'Brien was arrested on 5 August at Thurles and was sent to Kilmainham Gaol. He was tried at Clonmel on 28 September, and was found guilty of high treason. On 9 October he was sentenced to be hanged, drawn and quartered. Later the queen commuted the sentence into transportation for life.

In Hungary, the early military successes of the revolutionary army were halted by Prince Windischgraetz, the new army commander of the Austrian forces, and by December 1848 he occupied the capital. Still, the revolution was not defeated. The Hungarian government, now headed by Kossuth as governor, retreated to Debrecen, to the east of the country, and the best part of the army, under General Görgey, retreated and regrouped in the mountains in the north.

In 1849 only two countries held out against the tide of political reaction and reactionaries: Venice, under Manin, and Hungary in Kossuth's and Görgey's hands. Like Piedmont earlier on, Venice was soon crushed by the military might of Radetzky (known to most people nowadays, by the rousing march composed by Strauss). But Hungary, while facing Austria only (that is before the Russian intervention), had a fantastic resurgence. Görgey's army came down the mountains in February, liberated the heart of the country in March and April and reconquered the capital in May. At that point the king, by then the young Francis Joseph, reminded the czar of the Holy Alliance of the 1815 Vienna agreement and asked his help. In June, July and August a Russian army from the east, and Radetzky's right hand, General Haynau, from the west defeated the Hungarians. A reign of Austrian terror ensued, with executions, beatings and direct rule without parliament.

This state of affairs elicited an immediate Irish lament in the form of a poem by Samuel Ferguson, entitled 'Hungary, August 1849', first published in the September 1849 issue of the *Dublin University Magazine* – a supplication to Almighty God to end the bloodshed in Hungary. Things began to improve in 1861. In September of that year an imperial parliament was summoned to Vienna. All the so-called provinces sent deputies – the Croats, the Czechs, the Silesians – but not the Hungarians. In Pest a new leader emerged – Ferenc Deák, a member of the landed gentry, and a constitutional lawyer. The Hungarians demanded to be given back their own parliament; at length the king consented. However, the first demand made by the parliament was for the restoration of the laws of 1848. In the gallery, watching and hearing this parliament to its last day, was William Smith O'Brien, sitting in the company of Count Béla Széchenyi, the reformer's son, who translated the gist of what was going on to the Irishman. First they spoke German to one another and then they discovered a common language, Latin.

O'Brien had come back to Europe from Tasmania in 1854 on account of his ill health. He returned to Ireland in 1856 but was bound to stay out of politics. In 1859 he visited America, while in 1860-1 he spent time in Paris and Vienna, finally ending up in Pest. We have six very legibly written volumes of his unpublished diaries in the possession of Anthony O'Brien, of Aylesbury Road, Dublin. I quote from the pages describing William Smith O'Brien visiting the last session of the Buda parliament in 1861: 'It was the best day of my life.'

Lack of time prevents me going into further details of O'Brien's delightful journal;² suffice to say that he concluded that the Irish should follow the pacific Hungarian path of Deák, having honourably failed at arms just as the military insurrection of Kossuth had failed.

Although I have studied Griffith, who drew the same comparisons, and expanded on them, I do not know how much of O'Brien's later views were known to him. Griffith had picked up the trails of the other Young Irelanders, Mitchel, O'Reilly (who had met Kossuth in exile) and Doheny, and their successors, like John Francis O'Donnell, one of the editors of *The Nation*. He wrote the poem '*Cui bono*', whose words could have been woven into all revolutionary banners, Irish or Hungarian.³

2 The entry for William Smith O'Brien in the *Dictionary of national biography*, states that only one representation of O'Brien's visage remained. This is not the case. In the Foynes Island home of his great grandson, Murragh O'Brien, a full-length portrait hangs in the dining room. Anthony O'Brien has another portrait at Aylesbury Rd., Dublin.   3 This lecture was first delivered on 15 April 1998 in the Hungarian Embassy, Dublin, and again on 15 March in the Deansgrange Library, Dublin.

3

Reports of the Easter Rising in the Hungarian press

Dear friends, ladies and gentlemen![1]

In the middle of the Great War, subsequently named World War I, the Irish – some 1500 of their extreme nationalists – led by the left wing of Sinn Féin, rose at Easter, and proclaimed the Irish Republic in Dublin. The events of the war and of the Irish rising are well documented and expertly analysed from all angles: from the point of view of the insurgents, from the British side, by apologists, and later, by more objective historians, and also by outsiders, that is by almost entirely unbiased observers and analysts. There is no observation, or investigation without some modicum of bias; the motivation to present or to write about a sequence of events presupposes that the presenter or writer has a standpoint, and that he is describing happenings to an audience that has a standpoint too, similar, but not necessarily the same as his. But there are degrees of prejudice, and one should endeavour to reduce it to a minimum.

Since the rising was a decisive event, which created a new phase in Irish history, and put a permanent thorn in the side of Britain, one may not expect any contemporary reporting of its events to be totally objective and to cover all aspects of the event. The reporters themselves were divided, according to the alliance their nation belonged to, or (if they were from another part of the world) according to their sympathies and aspirations.

In 1916 Hungary, as part of the Austro–Hungarian empire, was fighting the British (albeit indirectly), who were the enemies of their ally, Germany. The move of the Irish freedom fighters, and of Casement in particular, to obtain German arms for Irish insurgents, was not surprising; nor was Britain's swift brutality, to put down the revolt and execute its leaders, totally unexpected. In a war my enemy's friends are also my enemies, and an armed rebellion by British subjects of Irish origin could well be judged as an act of war.

1 A lecture delivered at the Conference of the Hungarian Irish Friendship Association, Budapest 10 June 1999, with supplementary research material added in August-September 1999.

Yet the reporting of the Irish events in Hungary reveals some unexpected points. First of all, even though that Hungary was a German ally at the time, and so it could be credited with 'official' Irish sympathies, the Hungarian press was remarkably respectful towards the British in general, and the Westminster parliament and the British government in particular. Magyar pressmen reacted to news stories coming straight from Dublin, or via London, or (in some cases) through the foreign press – Dutch, Swiss, German, Austrian, French, Italian and American. Despite the war there seems to have been little news censorship and even less news embargo. Reuters, MTI (the Hungarian News Agency), *The Times*, the *Kölnische Zeitung*, *Le Figaro*, the *Frankfurter Zeitung*, the *Gaelic American* and the reporters of Hungarian newspapers all covered the events.

With its partner Austria in the dual monarchy, Hungary in 1916 was a significant European power whose population reached 20 millions and whose territory covered over 300,000 square kilometres. According to the records of the National Széchényi Library, there were eighteen daily papers published at the time, eight in Budapest, the rest in the provinces, five of them in other languages than Hungarian. To my knowledge no Hungarian historical investigation has ever covered all these papers, and here we must be content with looking at a digest of three of the more, arguably the most important, daily papers. Our investigation will focus, therefore, on three central newspaper of the Hungarian press – *Pesti Napló* (Pest Diary), *Magyarország* (Hungary), and *Népszava* (The Voice of the People). These were influential papers, and two of them among the most objective papers at the time. The *Pesti Napló* stood at centre left, *Magyarország* at centre right, while *Népszava* was a moderately left-wing newspaper, having close ties with the Hungarian Social Democratic Party. Their editors in 1916 were Imre Liptai (*Pesti Napló*), Andor Szakács (*Magyarország*) and Ernö Garami (*Népszava*).

In our survey of the Easter 1916 reportage we move chronologically, describing the news items, and the stories of Irish events as they were reported to the Hungarian public. From the tone of their reporting it seems that the pressmen took three things more or less for granted. One was the vague knowledge of the Hungarian reading public on matters Irish.[2] Pre-1916 books in the two largest libraries of Budapest testify that Ireland was presented, by and large, as a sizeable rural beauty spot, a more or less peaceful Atlantic island at the western extremities of Europe, inhabited by Catholics, in the south, and Protestants in the north – both sets British, by nationality. The second point was that Britain's image as an empire, fair as any empire could be, was at that time pretty well untarnished in their eyes. The third point was the most important. Although the pressmen, or anyone else I know about, had no knowledge of Arthur Griffith's *Resurrection*, or the date of his

---

2 Even Arthur Griffith's *Resurrection*, a work dealing with Hungarian history for the purpose of a parallel, was unknown. Cf. p. 32, note 42.

founding the Sinn Féin organisation – which was to burgeon and split, and play such an important part in subsequent Irish history – it was known in Hungary that the Irish were an exceedingly freedom-loving people, and that they had attempted to shake off their shackles through revolts, revolutions, uprisings and conspiracies in the past. Hungarian historians, thinkers, politicians of the nineteenth century had visited Ireland, and written about it, as a country with aspirations similar to those of the then semi-colonial Hungary.

Hot news carries mistakes, and I shall not attempt to correct them, even when it comes to mispelt names of people, or towns, or chronologically misreported events. You shall have here press reports, despatches, retold stories, warts and all, which – with a shortcut – you may compare to accurate retrospective historical information presented by Mr Győző Ferencz, in his 'Easter 1916' lecture yesterday in this conference.

The first report in *Magyarország* (27 April 1916) is a combination of three news items dated the previous day, coming from Amsterdam, London and Geneva. The Amsterdam news summary described the occupation of the post office, *Stephans* Green. some of the main roads of Dublin, and the fight between the insurgents and British troops coming up from the Curragh camp. We have an account of British losses, as nine dead and eight wounded. The Hungarian paper's own correspondent, staying in Genf, told of Sir Roger Casement's capture, 'who had earlier on revealed that *Findloy*, English ambassador in Denmark, had hired an assassin in 1915 to murder him'. The London report gave a short account of Asquith's demands to increase the British military budget, and of the closed session in Westminster, which might have dealt with the Irish question too.

The same paper's next reported news item (27 April 1916) is taken from the *Corriera della Sera*, 26 April, via Lugano. It talks of British troops getting the upper hand on the rebels, who are reported to be still holding out, and occupying various districts. Further on, it relates Sir Roger Casement's attempt to land on Irish soil, with arms smuggled from Germany, his capture, and his transfer to London.

On 28 April 1916 *Pesti Napló*'s leader is entitled: 'The Irish Revolution': 'And here is the real importance of the Irish revolution in the context of a world war. It will not crush the English empire. But it will weaken the resolve of the state ... and it will influence the opinions of foreign powers, friends or foes.' Sinn Féin demands are reported at the conclusion of this very long article, as being just and timely, namely, the establishment of an Irish parliament, strong support for the revival of the Irish language, and continued fight for total independence. The anonymous writer translated the expression *Sinn Féin* into Hungarian as *Our own land*. It is obvious that he was unaware of Griffith's having 'borrowed' the notion from Hungarian history, and having modelled Sinn Féin on Kossuth's *Védegylet*, of 1843. Later writers came up with a better translation, and today Sinn Féin is referred to as *Mi magunk*, in Hungarian.

Magyarország, 28 April, takes up a despatch of MTI, originating in London, whereby military recruitment will not be made compulsory in Ireland; then it confirms British losses in Dublin, as fifteen dead, and twenty-one wounded, and estimates the losses of the insurgents at eleven dead. The paper's own correspondent transmitted a message from Rotterdam about the alleged attempt by Sinn Féin to blow up a train at Marlborough. The newspaper's comment is that there is an irreconcilable difference between the viewpoints of Sinn Féin and the supporters of Home Rule. The former group wants full independence.

Népszava of the same date quotes the text of the viceroy's communication to the British prime minister, Asquith, which may be summed up with the phrase, *the situation is under control*, and then comments on its contents. On the whole, the situation may be under control, since, apart from small disturbances in the country, the authorities seems to have quelled the rebellion, locked Casement up in the Tower of London, but (some rebels might still hold out) the correspondent did not know in whose hands the post office building in Dublin was at the time of reporting.

The tenor of the next day's full-page article is very different in *Pesti Napló* (29 April 1916): 'The Irish revolution spreads to the provinces' is the title, and it incorporates despatches from London, The Hague, Amsterdam and Lugano. The article refers to a sermon by the bishop of Kensington, on Easter Sunday, which attacked the war, Asquith, and the delay in implementing the Home Rule policy in Ireland. The anonymous writer comments on the number of Irish soldiers innocently taking part in a war, which is not their war, in an army which does not fight for their interests. Although the German weapons did not reach their goal before Easter in Ireland, some American guns and ammunitions did.

The *Népszava* article of the same date is entitled 'The Irish question'. It contains analysis and comment which is followed by a second article compiled from foreign reports and despatches. The 'Irish question' is a historical glance, highlighting the religious intolerance of the British, and the famine which decimated the Irish population. It berates Redmond, the leader of the Irish party in Westminster, who supported recruiting Irish soldiers for the war. Sinn Féin, ready to redress the historical injustices, finds an ally among the American Irish, sons and daughters of immigrants, or even grandchildren of the Irish once driven out of their land. 'A state of siege' is the general title of these combined reports. The final one states that General Sir John Maxwell has been given plenipotentiary powers to quell the rebellion in the whole of Ireland.

The reports in *Pesti Napló*, 20 April 1916, are given the general title 'The Irish revolution'. This covers events already reported elsewhere, but adds two sets of detailed information. The first relates to rebels still holding Jacobs biscuit factory building and one railway station; the second is an un-named eyewitness report about the barricades in the post office building, the Sinn Féin attack on *Dams* street, the rebels unsuccessful 'siege' of Dublin Castle, and the occupation of Sackville Street, and its immediate environment.

Magyarország, of the same date, arranges its jigsaw of reported events under the familiar designation 'Irish revolution' which, by now, seems to have been generally accepted by the Hungarian press. Telegraphic messages from London, Frankfurt and Rotterdam list the destruction of Liberty Hall, and criticism of the British government's attitude to Irish affairs and of Redmond's intention to travel to Dublin and speak against the rebellion.

April 30th being Sunday, it was expected that all papers published on Sundays would devote space and mental energy to report and comment on the Irish revolution. So *Népszava* devotes two and a half pages of news and comment (30 April 1916) to Irish matters. The information is marshalled under three sub-titles: 'The revolt is still alive', 'The suppression of the revolt is commanded by General French', and 'The lines of communications are still broken between Ireland and England.' The first set of information, coming via MTI, claims that there are several points in the country where disturbances were noted: Enniscorthy, Clonmel and Gorey. The second quotes *La Stampa*, saying that certain districts in Dublin changed hands again and again, and some are still in the possession of the rebels. The third is another eyewitness account (via Amsterdam) of the fight on Dublin's streets. 'Neither side shot at the civilian population'; Sinn Féin cut one thousand telephone and telegraphic wires and disrupted rail lines.

On Monday, 1 May 1916, *Pesti Napló* presents two stories related to the 'Irish rebellion'. The first is a summary of the *Gaelic American*'s accusation that it was President Wilson who had warned the English government about Casement's plan and the patriot's expected arrival in Ireland. The second is an account taken from the *Daily Mail*, 20 April, which, apart from events already recounted elsewhere, told of the battle for St *Stephan's* Green, and of an all-night battle in darkness, as the street lights had been smashed. The estimated number of rebels is twelve thousand.

Népszava, on the same day, uses the sub-title 'Dublin in flames', under the general title, 'Revolution in Ireland.' The most sensational news flash came from the Milanese weekly, *Il Secolo*, via Lugano, which claimed that 'the rebels captured the viceroy of Ireland'. The other news items transmitted by Reuters, state that Pearse on the rebel side had been wounded, and had surrendered along with his unit, while James Connolly was shot dead.

Magyarország, on the next day, 2 May 1916, and under the same headline, echoes two foreign newspapers, the *Westminster Gazette* from London, and the *Frankfurter Zeitung*. According to the first, 707 people were detained by the authorities, including Countess *Markievic*, and it would be weeks before calm was restored. The second news item relates to a story written up on 1 May in Frankfurt, which tells of Sir Henry Craig's proposal of the previous day in Westminster, calling for the dismissal of Lord Wimbourne, the viceroy, and Mr Birrell, the chief secretary, for having mismanaged the administration of the country.

On 3 May a front-page article salutes Ireland in the *Pesti Napló*. 'The song of the Irish bard' laments the military defeat of the revolution and prophesises (beyond the present set of repressive British measures) the dawn of Irish freedom. On the next day, the newspaper publishes a short report, received from Reuters, on the damage caused by the strife, and a very ambitious article, from the pen of Miklós Lázár, one of the leading Hungarian journalist of the day, entitled: 'The green banner of the Irish'. This remarkably clear and accurate analysis of Irish events states that despite the help given to revolutionaries by the Germans, they are 'no more the friends of German militarists than the friends of a Westminster rule'. Lázár looks back at the events of June 1914 when followers of Jim Larkin were at the receiving end of suppression; it notices Sir Edward Carson's 'changing Protestant stance', before and after the outbreak of the war, and then looks back at the policy of O'Connell, who (after the success of the Catholic emancipation campaign) attempted to extend his energies agitating to abolish the Union with Britain. But O'Connell had not the courage to go to the ropes, and after the 8 October 1843 mass gathering, that had been dispersed by the order of the viceroy, he was a spent force. In Lázár's opinion Sinn Féin was an inheritor of the ideas of Young Irelanders, and their courage will not fail.

'A new phase of the revolution' might be on the way, says the correspondent of *Magyarország* on 4 May 1916, on its front page. But when we get to page six of this issue we learn only about an incident in Fermoy and about the hunt for rebel weapons in Enniscorthy. *Népszava* of the same date echoes the same information.

'Freedom fight defeated – the Irish rebel leaders executed,' says the title of the front page article of 5 May in the *Pesti Napló*. The deaths of Pearse, Clark and MacDonagh are reported and lamented, and Casement's 'inevitable' forthcoming execution is forecast. The commentator regrets the resignation of August Birrel, who held his post for a decade, and had a reputation of mildness and equanimity.

Besides echoing the Irish news published in other papers, *Magyarország*, 5 May 1916, reports the 'Demonstration of the American Irish' and comments on it – the news coming via Berlin, originating in the Wolff News Agency, New York. The Irish associations of Massachusetts and New York condemned Britain's treatment of the Irish insurgents, and John Devoy, the publisher of the *Gaelic American*, is reported saying: 'No matter how many leaders were executed new ones will come along. The fight will go on until it succeeds.'

'The defeated Irish revolution – the work of revenge' is the title of *Népszava's* news despatches woven into an article on 6 May 1916, which – in addition information already noted – gives an account of the detention of Lord Donough-more, Richard Walter *Heley* Hutchinson. This is followed by an historical summary, entitled: 'The sufferings of Ireland – struggle against English oppression'. Here, the readers are treated to a digest involving *Dermod Max Murragh*, Cromwell, the Irish parliament of the late eighteenth century, O'Connell and his readiness to compromise, the Fenians, Parnell, the boycott against James *Boykott*, the *Fönix* Park murders. (Note, that the spellings are not so much mistakes than attempts at Germanisation.)

'The Irish martyrs' is the title of the 7 May composite article in *Népszava*, based on reports from Reuters, Amsterdam, the *Daily Mail* and Berlin. The foreign newspapers are reported to echo moderate English opinion which counselled restraint in dealing with rebel leaders. In Amsterdam they seemed to know that 179 buildings had been destroyed in Dublin. In Berlin they claimed that three thousand people had been detained in Dublin alone. *Magyarország*, of the same day, comes out with a few more details, under the heading: 'Revolution in Ireland – its executed leaders'. Plunkett, *Daily*, O'Hanlon and Pearse were shot dead, fifteen more insurgents were sentenced to ten years, one for eight years in prison. John MacNeil, Sinn Féin president, was arrested. Countess *Markivicz* had a life sentence of forced labour meted out to her. Next day, 9 May 1916, a full article deals with 'The countess in green dress'. This time her name is spelt *Marzkievicz*. She is presented as an Irish suffragette, theatrical but heroic, a Shakespearean figure, who should be set free. In the same day's issue of *Népszava* 'The Irish rising' article has two subtitles: 'The newspaper of the revolutionaries' and 'The Irish Republic'. The London *Daily News* of 6 May 1916, reproduced the front-page article of the *Irish War News*, 25 April 1916, which was reporting the events of Easter Monday. Népszava translated the text and reproduced it in Hungarian. It also reproduced, in truncated form, an article of the *New States-man* on Roger Casement which was sympathetic to the Irishman's calling and praised his courage. *Népszava* marvelled at British freedom that allowed such positive comments on an insurgent who fought against the state at the time of war.

In the following day the main heading is changed to: 'After the Irish revolution'. It deals with two topics. The first is Redmond's concern, expressed in the Commons, that further executions which will provoke 'anger and frustration' among the Irish population. The second topic details the recent sentences: four more leaders shot, other rebels sentenced to eight years (one), five years (three), three years (three), two years (two).

Published originally in the *New Statesman*, Bernard Shaw's article in defence of Roger Casement appears a week later, on 11 May 1916, in Hungarian translation in *Népszava*. On 16 May 1916 another translation of Shaw's article is published in *Pesti Napló*. This paper's 13 May issue published a date for the commencement of legal proceedings against Casement (15 May). *Magyarország*, 13 May, devotes a full-page article to Casement's capture, based on material published in *The Times* and the *Continental Times*.

British lower and upper house debates reverberate in the 13 May 1916 issues of *Pesti Napló* and *Népszava*. The former comments on the exchange of views between Dillon and Asquith on 12 May in the lower house, Dillon demanding the cessation of executions, Asquith listing the casualty statistics: 304 dead. 1315 wounded. *Népszava* reporting on the upper house debate, describes Lord Loreburn's criticism of the administration of Ireland, and his demand for a decent peace settlement.

On 14 May *Népszava* publishes an article entitled: 'The Irish language – struggle against the English oppressors.' From the way the very existence and the continuous rejuvenation of Irish Gaelic is introduced it is obvious, that apart from linguists, who might know something about the activities and achievements of Douglas Hyde and Kuno Meyer, the Hungarian reading public is totally unacquainted with the subject. The anonymous writer states that: 'Championing the Irish language will, one day, be the same as championing Ireland.'

The 15 May *Pesti Napló* front-page article is entitled: 'Work for the hangman in Ireland'. This piece starts with statistics: fourteen Irish rebels were executed, two more were sentenced to death, seventy three persons were imprisoned, and one thousand seventeen hundred and three were sent to exile. Dillon's speech in Westminster is paraphrased. He demanded the cessation of military rule in Ireland. *Népszava*, on the same day, takes a report from *Corriera della Sera* about Asquith's visit to Dublin. Beyond the obvious purpose of Asquith's meeting with General Maxwell, the Italian paper suspects that the British premier was attempting to bring about a concordat between Dublin nationalists and Belfast unionists.

'Casement's trial' is the title of the sixteen liner, a piece of news originating from 16 May, in London, transmitted by Reuters on the same day, and published on 17 May in the *Pesti Napló*. Casement's appearance in Bow street magistrate court was watched by a posse of British and foreign pressmen. The prosecutor started the proceedings by describing Casement's consular service. Massive solidarity with Casement was expressed in practically all the one hundred and twenty-one meetings of the American Irish, far and wide in America, reports *Pesti Napló*, 20 May 1916, using despatches of the Wolff Agency. Many of the American Irish leaders stressed that the British government had ordered the execution of prisoners of war, who were not murderers.

'Criminal case in Ireland' is the title of the *Pesti Napló* article, 21 May 1916, which is based on a despatch from Reuters. Sir Matthew Nathan, chairman of the Royal Commission on the Irish Rebellion, was reported as claiming the existence of a criminal conspiracy by rebels, in contrast to the loyalty of the vast majority of Irishmen in the British army, and other Irish subjects. The same issue carries another article with the familiar title: 'The work of the hangman in Ireland'. It is a news report based on a diet of foreign papers: (*Daily News*, *Le Temps*, and the *Morning Post*), each of which reported on the Royal Commission. In the first, Carson was alleged to have been interviewed by Lloyd George; the second expressed a desire for Asquith to listen to the advice Carson might give on the situation; the third commented that 'the majority in Ireland sympathised with the rebels', a statement which was also to be made on 26 May in Westminster, and then refuted there, by Asquith (*Pesti Napló*, 28 May, 1916).

The last article in May in *Pesti Napló* – and the last in the batch closely reporting on the Irish rising and its immediate aftermath, is entitled: 'About the wife of Count Markievicz' (31 May,1916). The paper's information is based on an unnamed source from Stockholm. The article paraphrases an account of Casimir Markievicz, describing his wife's family, her character and her interests. Born Constance Gore-Booth, Countess Markievicz came from a rich landowning family. Her father, Sir Henry, owned estates in England and Ireland. Constance had been well acquainted with the viceroy in Dublin as well as with members of the court in London. An able woman with many talents, she was a noted amateur actress, a painter, whose paintings were exhibited in Paris, a brilliant raconteur, and one of the best dressed women in Dublin. Drawn to Ireland by his wife, Count Casimir was directing plays in the Irish capital and was member of an artistic club, some of whose other members have just been executed. He was well acquainted with Joseph Plunkett, William Pearse, and Edward Daly, at a time when they were not yet involved with politics. Casimir and Constance Markievicz lived in an artistic milieu between 1904 and 1908. In 1908 Constance's interest turned to the politics of Irish nationalism. She began to work actively for Ireland's independence, and for the establishment of the republic. She also supported some of the workers' strikes by giving financial help to the workers' families. Constance being totally committed to the cause of Ireland, no one was really surprised to see her involved with 'grave matters'. All this proved very stressful to the count but, being a foreigner in Ireland, he could not influence his wife to give up her politics. When Constance had extended her extreme nationalism to involve the theatre, count Casimir gave up his position in Dublin. Count and countess became estranged from one another. In 1913 the count left the theatre, and as a correspondent of an English newspaper, travelled in the Balkans. Since the beginning of the war in 1914 Count Markievicz has had no news of his wife until the sad news of her arrest.

In his book *Oliver St John Gogarty*, Ulick O'Connor summed up the events of 1916, this way: 'As a whole, Ireland was opposed to the rebellion. The war had enriched the farmers and the merchants. Large numbers of families were in receipt of remittance money from the front. The insurgents were looked on, at best, as misguided idealists, at worst, as German agents. The executions, however, focused attention on the character of the men who had taken part. They died with dignity. The three soldier-poets, men of priest-like purity of purpose, with strong elements of mysticism in their make-up, in particular caught the public imagination. The blood sacrifice which each had made could have been understood in fourteenth-century England or France; but in the twentieth century only in Ireland could it have had an effect. The executions of 1916 opened secret reservoirs in the national mind. They wore eventually to lend the people a purpose as fervent as that which inspired the Crusades or the pilgrimages of Peter the Hermit.'[3]

Let us now conclude this lecture with a piece of anecdotal evidence. An old friend of mine, Dr István Gál, the anglicist, and literary historian, said once, that Britain was a great nation whose only political mistake was the mistreatment of another great nation, the Irish; eventually that resulted in the first crack in their empire.[4]

3 Ulick O'Connor, *Oliver St John Gogarty* (London, 1964), p. 163.
4 Suggestions for further reading:
   Piaras Béaslai, *Michael Collins* (Dublin and Cork, 1937, Chapters 1-2)
   Csilla Bertha and Donald E. Morse eds. *Essays on Irish literature* (Debrecen, 1994, pp. 153-178)
   Owen Dudley Edwards and others, *Celtic nationalism* (London, 1968)
   Darrell Figgis, *Recollections of the Irish War, 1914-21* (London, 1927)
   Sheila Lawlor, *Britain and Ireland, 1914-23* (Dublin, 1983)
   Michael McKeown, *The greening of a nationalist* (Dublin, 1986)
   Magyarország, Hungarian daily paper, Budapest, April-May 1916
   Népszava, Hungarian daily paper, Budapest, April-May 1916
   Ulick O'Connor, *A terrible beauty is born: the Irish troubles: 1912-22* (London, 1975)
   Pesti Napló, Hungarian daily paper, Budapest, April-May 1916
   William Butler Yeats, *Dramatis personae 1896-1902* (London, 1936).

4

The Hungarian reception of Irish Independence and of Griffith's 'thesis', 1918-1944[1]

Professorial and student friends of Ireland, ladies and gentlemen!

At the beginning of my Griffith research in 1986 I enquired about the existence of *The Resurrection of Hungary* in Hungarian libraries. I had then only one positive report: the 1918 edition was held by the Széchényi, the Hungarian National Library. In 1998 and in 1999 I made a more thorough search personally: a copy of the same edition existed in the Szabó Ervin (the Budapest Municipal Library), and also in the Kossuth Lajos University Library of Debrecen. These volumes were acquired in the 1918-44 period, which is the time-frame of my present theme: how was Irish independence in general, and Griffith's thesis in particular, received at the time in Hungary?

The nature of every piece of historical research is such that – although it tries to be factual and objective – it has some declared, or undeclared purpose, presenting a historical picture that either relates to present-day events, or even better, shows a continuity from past to present. My topic is fortunate in more than one sense: some of Griffith's ideas had matured, had come to fruition, or had undergone a vehement change over the years, and his historical 'parallel' had a resurgence in the 1990s. Today both Géza Jeszenszky (foreign minister in 1991) and Árpád Göncz, president of the Hungarian Republic, own a copy of the 1904 edition of the *Resurrection*, presented to them by their Irish counterparts in 1993 and 1995 respectively. With the notable exception of Ulster – which may also be on the road to integration – the island of Ireland is free, independent, autonomous, a success story of statecraft and economy, the den of the powerful Celtic Tiger.

1 With slight diversions – explaining some points of Irish history to Hungarian students – this lecture was delivered at two universities in Hungary, first on 23 February 1999 at Kossuth Lajos University, Debrecen and then on 24 February 1999 at the Institute of English and American Studies, Eötvös József University, Budapest.

One does not take away from the originality of Arthur Griffith by pointing out that the thought of a comparison between Ireland and Hungary was already to be found in the mind and in the diaries of William Smith O'Brien, though in an embryonic form. Drawing parallels and comparisons must have come readily to educated men of the last century: the prototype was, of course, Plutarch, but Giambattista Vico poured new wine into old skins later, and the historical ideas of Montesquieu had reverberated both with Vico's ideas and Plutarch's notions. And then, contemporary with O'Brien, there was Imre Madách, the Hungarian thinker and playwright In the works of the above-mentioned authors, comparisons were made showing developments on not too dissimilar lines, in the life of different nations, and it was claimed that beyond that conception the forces shaping local history were also identical. If world history were a slice of the great oak tree of nature, individual national histories could be circles of yearly growth in that tree. It is, therefore, not really surprising that a notion which had already taken root by the end of the last century, namely, that oppressed nations must shake off their shackles by the rejuvenating forces of nationalism, could be readily applicable to Hungary and Ireland in terms of historical comparisons.

My lecture poses two main questions: how was Irish independence received by contemporary Hungary, and did the 'parallel' recognised by Griffith at the turn of the century continue to be a conceptual reality in the 1930s and '40s?

Without having done genealogical research on Irish families settled in Hungary, I can only quote letters and anecdotal evidence by those who claim Irish ancestry there. Some trace their forebears back to the Cromwellian persecution – such as the Egan, Murphy, Kelly and Kenedi families (the last is the Hungarian version of Kennedy); others, like the Fallon, Maher, O'Brien, and the Martyn families migrated more recently and have nineteenth and early twentieth-century Hungarian connections. This small kernel of the Hungarian-Irish might have helped in boosting the Hungarian response to the Irish renaissance, otherwise known as the Gaelic Revival.

Playing the *advocatus diaboli*, we may account for some vital dissimilarities between that country and people in the West, and the Magyars with their landlocked country in central Europe. Taking the 1918-44 period, the population of the island of Ireland was barely over five million; that of Hungary – after the Trianon Treaty which shrank the country to one third of its previous size – was not quite ten million. The Irish mainly spoke English – only five per cent of them spoke Irish – both Indo-European languages; the Magyars spoke Magyar, a Finnougrian language.

Where was, where is the parallel?

It was first and foremost in the political and intellectual oppression which was the outcome of the British domination in Ireland, and the Austrian domination in Hungary. Looking back at the pre-1867 era in these two countries, the miseries seem really comparable, and some of the causes of these miseries too. Then extricating itself from tutelage, from 1867 onwards, and up until late 1918, Hungary was a partner in the Austro-Hungarian empire; it shared with Austria a king, many political institutions and economic prosperity. This was the Hungarian model for Griffith, and for this second resurgence in the Hungary of the *Ausgleich* era he used the grandiose phrase: 'Resurrection'. Griffith, in his book, and in subsequent articles in the *United Irishman*, and the *Sinn Fein Weekly*, had been hinting at other aspects of social and religious comparisons, such as the domination of the Catholic Church in both countries, and the general background of Christian culture, but he never exploited literary comparisons, or the important role music played in the maintenance of sentiment sustaining ideas of independence, and in keeping alive historical traditions. He was more than aware of the Irish ballad heritage but not of its Hungarian counterparts or its chief exponent, János Arany. He loved the Magyar novelist Mór Jókai, whose works he could read in English translations, but knew nothing of Kálmán Mikszáth or, for that matter, of Hungarian poetry after Sándor Petöfi. There were no translations of Endre Ady, who was not only a contemporary of W.B. Yeats but probably his equal in poetic power and inspiration – a fact, alas, undemonstrable to the Western world because his poems were written in an esoteric language, Hungarian.

It is notoriously difficult to recognise the stature of contemporaries. One can hardly blame Griffith for not knowing that James Joyce was a genius, and that Gyula Krúdy was one too; both wrote poetry in prose. Similarly, the (emergent) comic talent of Flann O'Brien was not dissimilar (seen in hindsight) to that of Frigyes Karinthy, the most outstanding Hungarian humorist of all time. It is often said: 'the smaller the country the larger its postage stamps'. But this says little about a nation's spirit, because the more fervent it is, the more incisive talents it will produce.

Perhaps the most penetrating example of Griffith's insight was his recognition of the two ways in which both the Irish and the Hungarian nation had been – and have been – reacting to cataclysmic events in their history. At given times, both would take up arms and the respective public opinion of the day would approve military confrontation. However, when the odds seemed to be against armed struggle, the mood of peace and reconciliation would prevail in both countries. And yet, *at any time*, there were, and are, advocates of either the forceful or the peaceful methods, and no sequence of events could convince the advocates of arms that their approach was too brutal, unnecessary or untimely. Nor could one persuade the devotees of peace and compromise that military or paramilitary methods would work in the long run.

Griffith's biographers refer to the *Resurrection* as a political meteorite on the Irish night-sky of the beginning of this century. But, *The Philosophy of Irish*

Ireland, a book by D.P. Moran, was a comparable publication at that time. The articles forming the book were published in 1905. Like Griffith, Moran was also a member of Cumann na nGaedheal, which had adopted some of Griffith's policies, starting with the famous 1902 proposal to withdraw support from the Irish Party at Westminster, unless they could muster as much courage and opposition as the Hungarians had showed in their parliament of 1861. Moran was in full agreement with this policy and advocated the casting off of the British cloak and becoming, once again, fully Irish. In the immediate future of Ireland Moran foresaw the battle of the two cultures, the Pale and the Gael, and prophesised total Irish victory with the help of the Irish language. For all that, his book was written in English.

There were two outstanding Hungarian political analysts, József Eötvös in the nineteenth, and István Bíbó in the twentieth century, who observed and analysed what they considered 'the Irish question'. The title of Eötvös' study was *Poverty in Ireland* – indeed, poverty *was* the main problem in the last century; Bíbó, on the other hand, offered some insights relating to the problems of the North. Here I would just like to call attention to the existence of these studies without detailing them. Both of these analysts came from the 'peace camp' and their general attitude of nationalism may be summed up by two statements of József Eötvös (in his book on the influence on the state of the leading ideas of the nineteenth century): 'Nationalist tendencies may triumph but this will not necessarily satisfy Europe …Should nationalism be other than breaking the shackles of foreign oppression … that other must be grabbing power.' In other words, Eötvös foresaw the potentially ambivalent forces of nationalism.

Other political thinkers offer justifications and some apologies for nationalism. One of the first 'sacred scriptures' on nationalism is to be found in Mazzini's *I doveri d'uomo* (1844), which fully justifies nationalist aspirations, linking them with the right of self-determination. This prophetic foresight presaged the late twentieth-century declaration on human rights by the United Nations, but it also opened the floodgates, whereby no people seems to be small enough, nowadays, to aspire to nationhood, thus breaking up states and dismembering countries.

According to Engels (and then the whole Marxist school), nation states were formed at the sunset of feudalism. And according to Christopher Hill, and the majority of English historians, Cromwell was a progressive, a champion of parliamentarism. In truth, matters are never so simple, never so one-sided. Nation states were emerging all over in Europe *while* feudalism was still reigning supreme, and Cromwell – whatever else he was – had no respect for any nations or nationhood other than his own.

In the last thirty years there have been many attempts to classify the types of nationalism and outline their evolution. My personal favourite is *Nationalism and the State* (1982) by John Breuilly, who seems to have digested A.J.P. Taylor's main views and opinions as well as many other informed statements by other historians. In Breuilly's categorisation both the Irish and the Hungarians belong to the class of 'separatist nationalism'. In the nineteenth century Hungarian nationalism came first, with a programme which Kossuth was to carry out with arms, at first without accepting the (similar) programmes of other people living in Hungary are in the regions surrounding the Magyars. In other words, Croatian, Romanism and nationalism was largely ignored. A modified version of the original programme was incorporated in the statues of the Dual Monarchy, and it prevailed between 1867 and 1918. The first major action of modern Irish nationalism was the 1798 rebellion. These were the twin lodestars of Griffith's banner: the success of the Austro-Hungarian monarchy (in terms of nationhood and Hungarian nationalist aspirations) and the programme of the 1798 Irish rebellion.

In Griffith's plans for the future the language question was an important but not the most important issue. In Breuilly's judgement the Irish language was not the vital defensive weapon in fighting the British: the bastion of Catholicism was already the main defence. On the other hand, Hungarian nationalism was, and is, language-based. Echoes of the poet Ferenc Kölcsey's dictum 'A nation lives in its language' reverberate even today; this was first announced in the Hungarian parliament of 1825 and a thousand times since.

In Breuilly's view there was a parallel between Irish and Hungarian society in so far as both were agricultural, and even farm-dominated up until the end of the Second World War and somewhat beyond. In Hungary the national institutions, and especially the administrations of the countries, were fortified by parliament. Although Irish aspirations were similar, the institutions and the local attitude to them had to go through a slow decolonising transformation. And finally (and I would say, above all) there is the specificity of the 'Hungarian model' which included the apotheosis of Magyar culture. I am sure that this last point is equally true of Irish nationalism, and, more or less, of the nationalisms of other peoples too: they all prioritise their own culture. The success of Irish literature written in the English language proves that English as a mother tongue could carry Irish cultural genes. The theory behind it was emblematically expressed by Hugh Maxton *verba voce*: 'Literature is the Irish ideology.' As for literary practice, four names would do: Yeats, Shaw, Beckett and Heaney.

Before outlining the Hungarian reception of Irish independence, let us glance at three books of Irish history, one or the other of which is known to Hungarian students of Irish studies. (There are such courses at Budapest, Debrecen and Pécs, and some relevant studies in Szeged, too.) The works in question are: *Ireland in the Twentieth Century* (1974) by John A. Murphy; *Twentieth Century Ireland* (1994) by Dermot Keogh; and *The Restless Dominion* by David Harkman. Our era is divided into five periods by Murphy, and the other two authors more or less concur. For further reference these are: 1. The struggle for independence,

1919-21; 2. The Treaty and the Civil Wars, 1921-3; 3. The Irish Free State – under Cosgrave; 4. The triumph of de Valera, 1932-8; 5. Neutrality, from 1939 onwards. In short, the treatment is naturally positive, though Murphy, Keogh and Harkman do not gloss over mistakes. Modern Irish history in their treatment is a home brew: the Irish drink the soup they cook. The basis of the Anglo-Irish Treaty of 1921, which divided Ulster from the rest of the island, was the pressure Lloyd George successfully applied: Griffith and his divided delegation finally caved in. This was, however, the price the Irish had to pay to open the way to full independence in the rest of the island.

It is instructive to see what the adversary says. For that reason I examined the treatment of Ireland in three English history books currently used in English universities. These were: W.N. Meddlicott, *Contemporary England, 1914-1964* (London, 1967); R.K. Webb, *Modern England* (London, 1969); and Keith Robbins, *The Eclipse of a Great Power*, 1870-1992 (second ed., London, 1994).

Meddlicott's emphasis in describing Irish events is on its financing by the American Clár na Gael. Describing the Easter rising, he points out that only 1500 Irish soldiers fought in it while there were 135,000 Irishmen fighting in the Great War on the side of the English. His periods are entitled: 1. Home Rule; 2. Dominion Status; 3. Free State; 4. Éire. The crunch in the matter of the division came in July 1920 when de Valera and Sir James Craig of the North signed an armistice. The 1921 Treaty was based on that. Meddicott traces the steps to full sovereignty and independence which dates only from 1949, the solemn declaration of the Republic of Ireland.

In Webb's treatment of the Troubles, the English auxiliaries and the IRA are equated as unacceptable extremists, both operationally and on moral grounds. Robbins calls attention to the fact that the Easter rising was meant to involve Casement's German weapons, and since the latter ended up at the bottom of the sea, the rising ought not have happened. In Robbins' view the Council of Ireland was to have harmonised decisions by the Northern parliament with that of the Dáil. Although that body dissolved in 1925, it was the prototype of the Anglo-Irish agreement of 1986.

Our attempt to register the Hungarian reception of Irish events is the first of its kind, and it cannot claim completeness. My researches were restricted by time and place: three visits of short duration to Hungary, and the examination of readily available sources in the Hungarian National Library, the Budapest Municipal Szabó Erwin Library and the County Library of Székesfehérvár which houses the Géza Supka collection of international press cuttings. (The 'Hungarian collection' of the Irish National Library and Maynooth are about 50 works each; there are about 500 Hungarian-related books in Trinity, and also in the library of the Hungarian embassy in Ireland, and three times the total in my own private library in Newcastle, Co. Dublin.)

The lion's share of the Hungarian interest was in Sir Roger Casement, his actions, his martyrdom and his anniversaries. Although expert historians have committed an understandable error in calling the older Casement 'British' (he was indeed a 'British' subject and had a British passport, which he loaned, at least once, to a Hungarian escapee), the publicist of the *Nemzeti Újság* in 1941 knew him to have been an Irishman, father to Roger Casement, the executed patriot. Although the anonymous writer and other commentators did not seem to know about Sir Roger Casement's own article in the 1905 *United Irishman*, they were, nevertheless, aware of the essentials of the father's story which inspired the son to be both a Hungarophile and a fighter for Irish freedom. The 3 May issue of *Népszava*, for the twentieth anniversary of the younger Casement's death, recounted how the older Casement helped Kossuth in 1849 and how the younger Casement was ready to sacrifice everything – career, reputation, life – for the sake of Irish freedom. As a writer and reader of the *United Irishman*, the younger Casement must have read the life story of Petöfi in its 24 December 1904 issue. In that Arthur Griffith (using the unusual pseudonym of 'Carganac') described the ultimate sacrifice of the Hungarian poet on the battlefield. Some of Casement's early role-models were Hungarians, and the Hungarian reception of Casement's sacrifice was positively influenced by the 'parallel fates' of executed Hungarian generals in 1948, and the death of Sir Roger in 1916.

The writer of the *Népszava* article knew that in 1914 Casement wrote a pamphlet against recruitment in the Great War, and he was aware of the Irishman's visit in 1915 to Berlin, to obtain arms for a forthcoming rebellion. We may insert here an interesting and hitherto unknown episode: in the same year Casement visited Munich too, where two portraits were painted of him, one of which was acquired by Séamas Ó Síocháin, Casement's biographer (1995), and now hangs in his Lucan home.

There were three other significant articles published in the Hungarian press, namely in *Magyar Nemzet*, 21 October 1933, in *Pesti Napló*, 30 July 1939 and in *Nemzeti Ujság*, 17 August 1941, on various aspects of the Casement story. The first dealt with the report of a Hungarian detective, called Móric Fischer, who had claimed to have proved that Casement was betrayed by an American journalist in 1916. The *Pesti Napló* article was written by Jenö Szatmári, who had traced back the unfortunate turn of events to a briefcase stolen from a German diplomat by a British agent which had contained evidence against the Irishman. The third article, praising the achievements of the younger Casement, gave a summary of his father's exploits too, thus correctly identifying him as an *Irish* patriot. One should add to all this, that according to an article in the *Irish Times* of 27 January 1999 the British had endeavoured, already in 1915, to assassinate Casement, whom they considered, because of his German connections, extremely dangerous. Documents from MI5 suggest that the British consul in

Norway promised £5,000 to Christensen, one of Casement's friends, to assassinate the Irishman. We will have seen in the previous chapter of this book that Casement's fate was the subject of many Hungarian press reports in 1916.

In our period there were four popular books written in Hungarian about independence-seeking and then independent Ireland. István Bernáth, *Az ír szabad állam* (1932) is an enthusiastic but incomplete account of the history of the Irish Free State; this book can still be found, but only in the largest Budapest libraries. Zoltán Keszthelyi, *Irország* (1942) is a handsome and accurate summary of Irish history with a text of 150 pages, more than half of which is devoted to the 'five periods' of Murphy, with particular attention to the last period: neutrality; the book was published under the aegis of the Hungarian Social Democratic Party, whose organ was the *Népszava*, which – at the time – was as supportive of peace as it was possible to be in Hungary, at that time fighting a losing war on the side of Germany. The books by Lajos Egan, *Irország* (1905) and János Csuday, *Irország* (1910), are unremarkable.

Following the reports of the Hungarian press, especially between 1923 and 1944, it is possible to gain a somewhat disjointed, yet still fairly factual, story about the gradual emergence of Irish freedom. Articles in the *Pesti Napló*, October 1923, and January 1928, make cursory reports, one about the constitution of the new Irish government, the other about the death of William O'Brien. However, the most interesting and detailed article in the journal was published on 14 April 1935 about de Valera's policy. I quote from the concluding paragraph of the long and well informed article: 'The Hungarian language reform is now paralleled in Ireland. This is no coincidence: the Irish war of independence was sparked off by Hungarian example. Irish self-respect and enthusiasm caught the flames of a revolutionary pamphlet which had recounted the Hungarian events of the nineteenth century'.

I. Sós, the well-informed and liberal political columnist of the *Magyar Hírlap* (a journal of the political centre-left) published an article on 4 May 1937 on 'Ireland', *apropos* that as a 'free, autonomous and independent state' it was in the enviable position of being able to choose an ally without undue pressure from either the former colonial power, or Europe's largest emerging force. On the following day – 5 May – the political column gives an account of the new Irish constitution with considerable enthusiasm and envy. It was implied, if not expressed, that Hungary was sliding fast towards a humiliating alliance with Germany with internal right-wing forces fawning on Nazism, while Ireland, under de Valera's leadership, was steering clear of the muddy waters of large powers. Four days later, on 9 May 1937, Lajos Gosztonyi, a well-known and well-respected liberal, writing in the same journal, expressed his disapproval of the Irish Blueshirt movement. He went to the trouble of writing a long preamble to his disapproval, a kind of historical survey of Ireland, well-meaning but inaccurate, which was to illustrate that the Blueshirt movement was somewhat alien to Irish historical tradition.

The 9 July 1937 article in the *Pesti Napló* is unsigned, which is unfortunate, since the author had come up with a set of interesting and unusual information. The article was entitled: 'Ireland in labour' ('Irország vajúdása'). The anonymous writer described – in a summary fashion – the eleven years of Ireland's history since the struggle for independence, with a view to presenting the new Irish Constitution as progressive, well thought out, in a word: (once again) *enviable*. The writer then informed his readers of a gift: the 1904 edition of *The Resurrection of Hungary*, sent to him by 'Lord Plunkett', a book which he found fascinating. His summary description of the contents of Griffith's work is excellent and obviously the first serious notice of the book in Hungarian. Finally, the reader could also learn that there was some partial reciprocation from the Hungarians, since a lady, called Zsuzsanna Kemény, was going to give lectures in Dublin. (In time I hope to trace her steps.)

The 9 April 1939 article of the *Magyar Nemzet* had four columns devoted to Ireland. The anonymous writer gave another short historical survey of events but with a different emphasis: he described the role of the American Irish in influencing and financially aiding twentieth-century developments in Ireland. As for the cause and motivation for it, he traced back American-Irish commitment to Irish immigration to America in the last century. Finally he discussed the animosity between Ireland and England in 1938, when de Valera was again leaning on the IRA to get results. The writer of the article put his faith in the permanence of Irish neutrality, and stated in conclusion: 'Even the greatest nation cannot trust its own power in the long run to ignore the rights of smaller ones.' There were further reverberations in the 1 June 1939 and the 16 June 1939 issues of the same paper, each striking the same keynote.

With hindsight it is not difficult to see that these writers in *Magyar Hirlap*, *Pesti Napló* and *Magyar Nemzet* were quoting or even 'boosting' the Irish stance of neutrality, at a time when Hungarian neutrality was in great danger of being 'rubbed out' by German politics. Alas, Hungary had already entered the war, on the German side, when on 1 December 1940 a brave and talented MP, Miklós Kállay, wrote an article in the *Nemzeti Ujság*, entitled: 'The secret of the Green Island' ('A zöld sziget titka'). Apart from its seminal content this is the most poetic article that has ever been written about Ireland in Hungarian. Kállay's exposition starts with Cromwell's bloodbath, and the Irish reaction to it: emigration and resistance. He also depicted the famine, particularly the year 1845, and surmised that the afflicted reacted to it, again, in a similar way: by emigration and by inner resolve, which helped them to survive. According to Kállay the 'secret' of the Irish is in their innate capacity to resist pressures. This ability was helping them to refuse the alternate pressures and enticements of both the English and the Germans wooing them to enter the war on either of the two sides. The 29 January 1942 issue of *Nemzeti Újság*, and the 29 August 1942 and 11 October 1942 issues of *Magyar Nemzet*, were equally eloquent in singing the praises of the Irish for having refused to budge.

The last Hungarian communication in our period about Ireland was an official news item, taken from the Reuters News Agency which stated in October 1944 that Irish neutrality was and remained impartial; Ireland had refused to force the representatives of Germany to leave the island.

Instead of a summation, let us look beyond this paper. One ought to examine Irish Hungarian relations from the end of the Second World War to 1989, the beginning of newly found Hungarian freedom. The mutual sympathies continued, the contacts became more frequent. In terms of a literary bibliography one ought to continue the work of Gizella Kocztur, *Irish Literature in Hungarian Translation* (Budapest, 1971).

The great challenge for the present is the membership of the European Union: the opportunities it offers to Ireland, and the future prospects it might provide for Hungary. It is now a question of how to learn from the Irish; not just the exploitation of available structural funds but the modes of positioning a small nation amidst greater economic powers. Since 'the affinities' are there, between a Western European and a Central European people, the exchanges will multiply; a steady stream of Hungarians will have their 'Irish schooling' – engineers, farmers, biologists. There is currently a 'Hybernomania' in Hungary, and the Irish reciprocate with excellent hospitality in their own land. (But then, it is easier to love a distant friend than a close neighbour.)[2]

2 Suggestions for further reading:

Endre Ady, Hungarian poet (1877-1919), translation in: Joseph Reményi, *Hungarian writers and literature* (New Brunswick, N.Y., 1964)

János Arany, Hungarian poet (1817-1882): some translations in: Thomas Kabdebo ed., *Hundred Hungarian poems* (Manchester, 1976)

Philip Caraman, *The years of siege: Catholic life from James I to Cromwell* (London, 1966)

József Eötvös, Hungarian statesman (1813-71); his novel *The village notary* (London, 1851) is the only work translated from him.

Christopher Hill, *God's Englishman: Oliver Cromwell and the English Revolution* (London, 1970)

Mór Jókai, Hungarian novelist (1825-1904): for works see p. 41, note 75.

Frigyes Karinthy, Hungarian humourist (1887-1988), *Journey around my skull* (London, 1939)

Ferenc Kölcsey, Hungarian poet and politician (1790-1838), the author of the text of the Hungarian National Anthem, bilingual edition: Edition Plurilingua (Budapest, 1998)

Gyula Krúdy, Hungarian novelist (1878-1933). *The red stagecoach*, translated by Paul Tábori (Budapest, 1962); *Sinbad,* translated by George Szirtes (Budapest, 1997)

Imre Madách, Hungarian playwright (1823-64); his masterpiece is now available in a good translation: *The tragedy of man*, translated by George Szirtes (Budapest, 1993)

Randal McDonnell, *When Cromwell came to Drogheda: A memory of 1649* (Dublin, 1906)

Giuseppe Mazzini, Italian politician (1805-72), *Life and writings of Joseph Mazzini* (London, 1864-70). 6 vols

Kálmán Mikszáth, Hungarian novelist (1847-1910). Latest translation: *The grass of Lohina* translated by Bernard Adams (Budapest, 1997)

Charles-Louis de Secondat Montesquieu (1639-1775), *L'esprit des lois* (Paris, 1748)

William Smith O'Brien, Diaries Mss. for the year 1861, the custody of Anthony O'Brien

Sándor Petöfi, Hungarian poet (1823-49), translations of his poems in: *The miracle stag*, an anthology of Hungarian poetry, ed. Adam Makkai (Chicago, 1996)

Plutarch, *Lives of the noble Grecians and Romans*, translated by Sir Thomas North (London, 1579)

Giambattista Vico (1668-1744) *La scienza nuova,* 4th ed. (Napoli, 1744, this is a posthumous and the first complete edition of his works).

5

Hungary and the two Roger Casements

Séamas Ó Síocháin and Thomas Kabdebo

INTRODUCTION

From an episode in the life of Louis Kossuth[1] which took place in 1849, Hungarian history and historiography knows about 'Roger Casement'. But contemporary writers[2] (like Kossuth and his circle) and later historians[3] took him to be an 'Englishman'. He was, in fact, an Irishman and the father of the well-known Irish nationalist, Sir Roger Casement (1864-1916), famous for his humanitarian activities in defence of indigenous peoples, and executed for his part in the 1916 Rising.[4] The understandable misidentification of Casement Sr. (1819-77) as an Englishman was also applied to other Irishmen active in Continental Europe, if for no other reason than that they all had British passports.

Casement's Hungarian adventure attained a certain significance in his son's life, as did the general Hungarian background of which it was part. The present chapter will look at the historical details of the 1849 event and at its significance, as well as that of the Hungarian example in general, for Casement Jr. But it may be best to begin with the episode itself and the way it was first presented to an Irish readership in the early years of the twentieth century by Casement Jr.

---

1 L. Kossuth, *Meine Schriften* (Leipzig, 1880), vol. 3, pp. 342-6.   2 Count Gyula Andrássy, Hungarian plenipotentiary to the Porte, wrote a letter to Arthur Görgey, commander-in-chief of the Hungarian forces, on 7 Sept. 1849, from Widdin: 'A másik angol meg Indiából jött hozzánk' (the other Englishman came from India), *Az emigrátió iratai, 17*, in I. Hajnal, *A Kossuth-Emigrátió Törökországban* (Budapest, 1927), p. 466.   3 Hajnal himself, and then every historian of the period after him, including the present writer: cf. Thomas Kabdebo, *Diplomat in exile* (Boulder, Col., 1979), pp. 62, 184.   4 General details of Casement's career can be found in his three most recent biographies: Brian Inglis, *Roger Casement* (London, 1973); B.L. Reid, *The lives of Roger Casement* (New Haven, 1976); Roger Sawyer, *Roger Casement, the flawed hero* (London, 1984).

KOSSUTH'S IRISH COURIER

In 1904 one of the leaders of the growing nationalist movement in Ireland, Arthur Griffith, wrote a series of articles drawing lessons for Ireland from the experience of Hungary. These first appeared in the *United Irishman* and were published subsequently as a pamphlet entitled *The Resurrection of Hungary*.[5] Shortly afterwards, on 25 February 1905, the *United Irishman* published a piece entitled 'Kossuth's Irish Courier'. The article, signed 'X', was, in fact, by Roger Casement Jr.[6]

The article gave details of an episode in the life of Kossuth, which he subsequently described in his *Memoirs*. It told how, following defeat at Világos, Kossuth and his followers found refuge at Widdin, in Turkish territory on the Danube. Fearing that pressure from Austria and Russia would lead to their extradition, it was suggested that Kossuth should send a letter to the British prime minister, Lord Palmerston, appealing for British diplomatic intervention. The difficulty was in ensuring the letter's safe and rapid delivery. At this point an unknown 'Englishman' appeared, announcing that he had 'come from India to fight for Hungarian freedom'. After a brief consultation, the letter was entrusted to him, a dramatic journey was made, and the letter was placed in the hands of Lord Palmerston. British intervention did save the Hungarian patriots. Not until years later did Kossuth learn the name of his helper, and again it was during a fleeting encounter on a train in the United States that a gentleman handed Kossuth a card bearing the name 'Mr Roger Casement', and in pencil underneath 'I handed to Palmerston the letter from Widdin.'

THE HISTORICAL EVENT

The service rendered to him by Casement, in handing an important letter to Palmerston, would not have been the only memory Kossuth had of Casement's activities. Casement's passport, too, seems to have had a particularly interesting journey in late 1849, either as divorced from its rightful owner, or as duplicated for the purposes of smuggling Hungarian nationals across the frontiers of the re-established Austrian empire.

Our main sources for the historical details of the Casement episode are the informants and the writers of memoirs, Mrs Kossuth, Mrs Pulszky, and the English journalist Charles Pridham. Fearing police spies, past and present, they were deliberately vague on vital clues.

5 The pamphlet in book form was first published in 1904. The most recent study, explaining its Hungarian connections is Thomas Kabdebo, *The Hungarian-Irish 'parallel', and Arthur Griffith's use of his sources* (Maynooth, 1988), in Hungarian: 'A magyar-ir párhuzam és Arthur Griffith történeti forrásai', *Századok* (1991), 3-4sz. 309-331p. 6 The article was subsequently published in H.O. Mackey, *Life and times of Roger Casement* (Dublin, 1954), pp. 13-18.

In October 1849, in the company of an unnamed Hungarian officer,[7] Mrs Theresa Kossuth, the ex-governor's wife, escaped from the clutches of the Austrian authorities (who were, incidentally, holding her children).[8] Mrs Kossuth travelled under the false name of Mary Smith, while her gentleman escort held a passport that had been made out in the name of Roger Casement.

Evidence shows that Casement, having visited Kossuth's camp in September 1849, went to Vienna and there conferred with the British ambassador, Lord Ponsonby. He then proceeded to London. (He might also have met Mrs Kossuth, personally, in the east of Hungary but for the fact that one go-between mistrusted him.)[9]

The early publication of Kossuth's letter[10] (or copy of his letter) in Britain seems to suggest that, having talked to Lord Ponsonby in Vienna in October,[11] Casement hurried on to London, where he met Palmerston. His meeting with the British foreign minister (otherwise unrecorded) must have taken place on or shortly after 9 October. On that date a copy of the letter was published in the London *Daily News.*

It is possible that, while Casement delivered the top copy of the letter to Palmerston, he handed over a second copy to Kossuth's ex-ambassador, Francis Pulszky, in London. Pulszky had direct access to the *Daily News*, which was a paper friendly to the Hungarian cause. Alternatively, the letter could have been given to the *Daily News* by Charles Pridham. While Casement was travelling to London via Vienna, Charles Pridham travelled to Turkey from Vienna. He may have received a second copy from Kossuth himself and conveyed that to the *Daily News.*

Meanwhile Ambassador Ponsonby assured his foreign secretary that the refugees were safe in Turkey, but requested an 'exercise of the fleet' to the Dardenelles to insure their safety.[12]

---

7 A captain of the infantry regiment (Theresa Pulszky, op. cit., p. 33).   8 Since 25 September 1849. One may include here two accounts of Mrs Kossuth's escape: one is by Emilia Hogl (later Mrs Robert Rombauer); the other is by Theresa Pulszky, based on her recollections of Mrs Kossuth's own story: Robert Rombauer, 'Egy magyar nö élete az emigrátióban', *Budapesti Szemle*, 1813, pp. 286-97; Theresa Pulszky: 'Escape of Madame Kossuth', in *White, red and black,* by F. & T. Pulszky (London, 1853), vol. 1, pp. 17-45.   9 If the conjectures were right, Casement, on the way back from Turkey, and Mrs Kossuth, going towards Turkey, could have made contact in the Banat, in late September 1849: Theresa Pulszky, op. cit., p. 34.   10 Kossuth to Palmerston, Widdin, 20 September 184: Hajnal, op. cit., pp. 482-6. cf. *Daily News*, London, 9 October 1849.   11 The date of Casement's arrival in Vienna (2 October) seems to be a conjecture by Hajnal (op. cit., p. 147) and it cannot be corroborated exactly. A correspondent of the *Daily News* and *The Times*, Charles Pridham, is in Vienna at around this time (Charles Pridham, *Kossuth and Magyar land*, London, 1851, pp. 199-200). His account of what took place and whom he met is deliberately obscure. He may have met Casement in Vienna, at the beginning of October and he may have conveyed Kossuth's letter directly to the *Daily News.*
12 Ponsonby to Palmerston, 9 Oct. and 15 Oct., 1849 (PRO FO 7/370).

At length, Mrs Kossuth and Mrs Pulszky reached safety well before Kossuth himself, who was interned in Turkey until the autumn of 1851. Mrs Pulszky joined her husband, the Hungarian plenipotentiary, Francis Pulszky, in the autumn of 1849 in London. Her journey may or may not have been aided by Casement himself,[13] but Pulszky seems to have also received letters from Kossuth, possibly via Casement.[14]

From the reports and correspondence of various Hungarian officers in Turkey (as related by Hajnal) it is possible to say that Casement arrived in Widdin before 7 September and left after 20 September. He may have been in Vienna at the beginning of October and he could have arrived in London before 9 October. It was possible at the time to cover the distance in eight days even between Pest and London.[15]

THE SIGNIFICANCE OF THE HUNGARIAN EXPERIENCE IN THE LIFE OF ROGER CASEMENT JR.

Why his father's Hungarian adventure and the Hungarian struggle for independence should have come to the forefront of Casement Jr.'s consciousness when it did, when he himself was forty years of age, must be assessed in the context of his career as a whole. The year 1904 marked the beginning of his intense concentration on Irish affairs, which lasted until his death in 1916.

The 1916 Easter Rising in Ireland, though commanding little popular support when it took place, set in motion a series of events, which ultimately led to the break with England and the establishment of the Irish Free State. More than anything else it was the execution of the leaders of the rebellion that transformed public opinion. Following courtmartials, fifteen were executed by firing-squad, at intervals, between 3 May and 12 May. The last of the leaders to be executed, on 3 August, was Sir Roger Casement, this time by hanging and after a much-publicised trial. Casement had been in Germany trying to win support for the planned rising and attempting to raise an Irish brigade from amongst the ranks of Irishmen who had enlisted in the British army and were then prisoners-of-war in German camps. Having failed to persuade more than a handful of the

13 It was Mrs Gustáv Emich who 'had acquired' a false passport for Mrs Pulszky, in the autumn of 1849 and accompanied her to England: ('Sz': Pulszky Teréz. *Hazánk s a Külföld*, 14 March 1867.) I believe that many of the answers lie in the Lansdowne family archives, alas not open to researchers. Lansdowne (Henry Petty, 3rd marquess of Lansdowne) had been helping the Pulszkys from 1849 onwards. We do not know who their contacts were.   14 This is, again, a conjecture of the author's. There were other 'Englishmen' trusted with secret or semi-secret messages who had visited Kossuth's camp. Apart from the aforementioned Pridham, there was Charles Frederick Henningsen (author and correspondent of the *Daily News)* and two captains, Longworth and Herbert.   15 Blackwell to Emery, Pressburg, 7 Jan. 1848: Thomas Kabdebo, *Blackwell Küldetése* (Budapest, 1990), p. 284.

latter to join him, and realising that only extremely limited amounts of arms and ammunition were forthcoming from the German authorities, Casement became convinced that to continue with plans for a rising was folly. He persuaded his hosts to permit his return to Ireland by submarine in an attempt to stop the rising. He was however, apprehended shortly after landing and quickly trans-ferred to Dublin and then London.

In contrast to the other leaders, Casement had spent most of his adult life outside Ireland, having had a distinguished career as a British consular official, serving in Africa and in South America. His fame principally derived from two special reports, the first, on atrocities perpetrated on the native population of the Congo Free State mainly in connection with the extraction of rubber; the second, on an even more gruesome episode in the Peruvian territory of the Putumayo River (a tributary of the Amazon), where the Indian population was decimated, again in the context of the rubber trade. It was following submission of this latter report that he received a knighthood. British fury over his treason was, accordingly, all the greater.

While Casement seems always to have been proud of his Irish identity and to have cultivated from his youth an interest in Irish history, during the early part of his career he also seems to have been able to reconcile this attachment with a commitment to the ideals of an expanding British empire. This seems clear from his writings while in the service of the British foreign office: the period of his first position in the colonial service in the (then) Oil Rivers Protectorate (1892-5), through his time as British consul at Lourenço Marques (1895-8), and at St Paul de Loanda (1898) – punctuated by his involvement in the Boer War – and, finally, during his Congo period, culminating in his Congo investigation (1903). A change seems to have begun during the Boer War, where he subsequently claimed to have been shocked at the treatment meted out to Boer prisoners. Certainly, by the time of his Congo investigation, his feelings of Irishness began to affect his attitude to colonial oppression in general and to the British empire in particular. Writing in 1907 to Alice Stopford Green, he said: 'Well, the (Boer) War gave me qualms at the end – the concentration camps bigger ones – and finally when up in those lonely Congo forests where I found Leopold I found also myself – the incorrigible Irishman![16]

A major consolidation of his changed attitude came about during a long period of leave, much of it spent in Ireland, which followed submission of his official Congo Report. He was influenced by a new vibrancy which manifested itself in Irish public life – in the language movement, in the cultural and literary movements, and in political life. It was at this point, during 1904, that Casement read Griffith's Hungarian articles. He was influenced by the lessons of the

16 NLI Ms. 10,464: Casement to Alice Green 20/4/07.

Hungarian experience, as outlined by Griffith, but he was also attracted to the Hungarian case for the personal reasons, discussed above.

Casement Sr. had died in 1877, when his son, Roger, was twelve, but he had often told the Kossuth story to his children, and it had clearly made sufficient impact on young Roger that he both remembered its details and was anxious to share it with an Irish audience. Kossuth had taken his helper to be an English-man, describing his behaviour as typifying the English 'character'. For Casement Jr., who had begun to believe that there was an affinity between Irish people and oppressed peoples elsewhere, because of shared historical experience, it was important that both his father's Irishness and his action in leaving India and the British army to help the Hungarian cause be recognised.

On his return to Ireland after an abortive consular posting to Lisbon, he wrote to his friend, Mrs Mary Hutton: 'The *Resurrection of Hungary* also came back from Lisbon – and I shall read it during my enforced convalescent leisure.' He went on to tell her of his father's Hungarian intervention, and continued: 'He used to tell me this story when I was a little boy – and then, long ago I came across it in a Review of Kossuth's book in a London paper. So the *Resurrection of Hungary* has a special interest to me.' Further statements in his letter reflect his mood at the time: 'I may some day do something for my country. Yes, any man – or woman – who loves Ireland would gladly go to the scaffold – or to any shameful end – to strike such a blow for Ireland's honour and right as the Hungarians did in '48.'[17]

Early in the following year, 1905, he referred to the Hungarian incident to several of his friends, including Alice Stopford Green, Kate ffrench, his brother Tom, and his cousin Gertrude Bannister.[18] Tom replied: 'I got the *United Irishman* and Hungary Pamphlet ... How similar Ireland is to Hungary but we have no men like Deáke (*sic*) and Kossuth. All the spirit seems to have been knocked out of poor Ireland and I am afraid they never will get the right men to lead them. It is such a pity.'[19]

Arthur Griffith had put forward the strategy of Deák, who represented the 'peaceful' alternative to Kossuth's 'forceful' ways, as a model for Irish imitation.[20] This involved an avoidance of armed revolution in favour of systematic passive resistance. Casement was excited, as he showed in a letter to his cousin Gertrude. England 'will find we can play a more dangerous game than any we have yet attempted – Passive Resistance on a gigantic, national scale. No taxes, no recruits, no public service in any department the passive resistance can influence – such shall be the reply of Ireland.'[21] One concrete way to withdraw Irish support for England would be to stop Irishmen enlisting in the English armed forces. With

17 NLI Ms. 8612, Mary Hutton Papers. R.C. to M.H. 15/12/04.   18 NLI Ms. 10464, R.C. to Alice Green, 34/2222/05; Ms. 13073, Kate ffrench to R.C. 25/2/05.   19 NLI Ms. 13076 (1/i) Tom Casement to R.C. 10/3.05.   20 Inglis, op. cit., p. 135.   21 NLI Ms. 13074 (2/ii) R.C. to

Alice Stopford Green, an ardent Irish nationalist, and Bulmer Hobson, a young man who had joined the Irish Republican Brotherhood in 1904, Casement helped to write an anti-enlistment leaflet which was circulated in Ulster.[22]

Casement's next consular appointment was in Brazil. Here another of the Hungarian ideas was given expression – that of the dual monarchy.[23] From the time of his first consular appointment in Lourenço Marques he had noted that exports from Ireland were not distinguished within the overall British statistics. Casement began to rectify this. By the time he reached Santos, not only did he give attention to Irish exports: he had official letterhead printed with the words 'Consulate of Great Britain and Ireland'.[24] As his biographer, Roger Sawyer, points out, he put the thinking behind this into words some years later, when addressing potential members of his Irish brigade in Germany: 'The King you serve is, in law, King of Great Britain and Ireland. There is not such person as the King of England in law.'[25]

CONCLUSION

His father's Hungarian experience enabled Casement Sr.'s more famous son to link Ireland's struggle for independence with that of Hungary and to identify his father's actions as those of an Irishman, who could identify with the Hungarian cause as one used to viewing the plight of oppressed peoples from the inside. The 'Irish-Hungarian' policy, as the Sinn Féin policy was sometimes called in its early days, played a significant part in Casement Jr.'s thinking for some time.

Gertrude Bannister. **22** Ibid. p. 136, and Sawyer p. 48, and note 15 p. 168. In *Ireland yesterday and tomorrow* (Tralee, 1968), Bulmer Hobson wrote: 'A four-page leaflet was issued and very widely distributed. In its first draft it was written by Alice Stopford Green; Roger Casement added a bit, and I added more.' The pamphlet was *Irishmen and the English army*, Dungannon Club Publication No. 1. **23** See Sawyer, op. cit. p. 61-2. **24** Ibid., p. 52. **25** Ibid., p. 62.

6

'Our hearts go out to them' :
Irish reactions to the Hungarian Rising of
1956[1]

The quotation in the title is from a speech by the taoiseach, Mr John Aloysius Costello, delivered on Monday, 12 November 1956 at Tullow. The full sentence reads as: 'Our hearts go out to them in their agony' (*Irish Times*, 13 November 1956). It refers to the Hungarian nation crushed by the second, and this time gigantic wave of Russian military invasion, which involved two thousand tanks, just as many as the Germans had taken to occupy France in the Second World War.

The Hungarian revolution was an event that began as a domestic effort for democratisation, continued as an armed struggle of insurgents, against state security police, and ended as an unequal war between the might of the Soviet Union and Hungary's freedom fighters. It invited the sympathy of the West, and its relief with food, medicine, and eventually shelter for the refugees who crossed the guarded and hostile borders in their tens of thousands. Although it was defeated on the ground, it lived on in spirit, until the time was ripe for freedom at the end of the 1980s. The crack made by the 1956 Hungarian revolution in the edifice of communism, and in the imperial wall of the Kremlin – which had embodied Soviet rule before 1990 – was never repaired, and, moreover, the Communist parties in the West had lost their credibility.

Ireland's share in relief, in spiritual ammunition, and in welcoming the refugees, was commensurate to its size, and economic capacity at the time. When examining the Irish contribution in 1956, that is between 22 October and 31 December of that year, I will follow three lines. The first hinges on the reportage of events, and with the immediate comments it invited; the second deals with

1 Fortieth anniversary lecture, delivered on 23 October 1996 at St Patrick's College, Maynooth. The talk was illustrated with slides, and memorabilia, such as a piece of the Stalin statue demolished in Budapest, 1956 – not reproduced here. This text, on the other hand, was enriched with further research sourced at the Irish National Library in the summer of 1999.

such diplomatic efforts, on behalf of Hungary, where the Irish could and did join in; the third introduces the refugee crisis with Ireland's welcome to several thousand refugees.

The fermentation that kept Hungary excited in the autumn of 1956 reached a high point on October 6,[2] when László Rajk, the former communist minister of the interior, and later a victim of a colossal construction-trial in 1949, was reburied as a 'true communist martyr'. On 22 October, the eve of the revolution, reformers within the Hungarian Communist Party proclaimed publicly that 'there were different roads leading to Socialism', which implied that Hungary need not follow the Soviet Union slavishly. This was reported as front-page news in the *Irish Times* of 23 October, when Hungarians in Budapest – and students in Szeged – already held sympathy demonstrations for Polish reforms. The Poles then seemed to be one step ahead, with their reformist leaders at the helm, and the Soviet army and navy threatening to invade them (*Irish Times*, 23 October). The Polish story was pursued intelligently in the *Irish Independent* (22, 24 October, 31 December). The first piece explained the nature of the quarrel with the Soviets: The Polish Communist Party had asserted its independence by returning to the key post of first secretary of the party, the once-purged Titoist, Wladyslaw Gomulka. Later, the readers had direct comments from the pen of W.T. Dobrezynski, former Polish minister to Ireland, whose end of the year article was entitled 'Year of fear for Russian Goliath'.

Necessarily, the Irish press, but the European press as well, was always one day behind the events, and this was also the case with radio transmissions, to begin with. Later, Western pressmen penetrating into Budapest – and some, like George Mikes,[3] in other parts of Hungary – enabled the BBC to transmit reports, in their late-night news bulletins – that had happened earlier on the same day.

On 24 October the *Irish Times* (front-page news), relying on reports of the BBC and MTI (the Hungarian News Agency), accurately summarised the starting point of the events of 23 October: 'The Budapest meeting was advertised as a gesture of sympathy and solidarity with the Poles, but it turned into a public mass demonstration for a similar Hungarian declaration of independence from Moscow.' The demonstrators demanded: a trial for Mátyás Rákosi, the ruling despot between 1948 and the summer of 1956; the return of Imre Nagy (prime minister of reform in 1953-4) to the helm; and many other radical reforms, to do with agriculture, Hungarian uranium mines, free elections.

It is difficult to say when a revolution starts, but in 1956 it was sparked off by a student march, which swelled into a general demonstration by the populace of Budapest, moving enormous crowds mainly to three focal points of the city.

2 October 6 is Remembrance Day in Hungary, commemorating the martyrs of the 1848-9 freedom fight.   3 George Mikes (1912-87) was a Hungarian journalist, who settled in Britain after the Second World War.

About a hundred thousand people demonstrated in front of the parliament, and listened impatiently to Imre Nagy's pacifying speech; nearly ten thousand went to the city park, and felled Stalin's giant bronze statue there, and several thousand others – mainly young people – demanded to be heard on the radio, demonstrating in Bródy street. This led to violence: the state police guards killed two demonstrators. The armoured division of the Hungarian army, ordered by the minister of the interior to disperse the crowd, handed over their weapons to them, and a siege of the radio building ensued. The Irish press (*Irish Times*, *Irish Independent*) reported other episodes as well on 24 October: Ernö Gerö, the communist leader, returning from a foreign visit, delivered an inflammatory speech on the night before; Russian tanks were called out[4] to quell the revolt, unsuccessfully. The tanks were challenged, telephone wires were cut, and Imre Nagy continued to appeal for calm.

The events of 24 October were on the front pages of the next day's newspapers (*Irish Times*, *Irish Independent*). A battle was waging for the possession of the radio building, elsewhere tanks were shooting rebels on the streets, and the Russians were reported (from Vienna) to have executed twenty eight of their soldiers who had refused to fight the rebels in Budapest. Let us note the vocabulary of reportage, not just in Irish newspapers. *Rebels* of the first few days became *insurgents* later, and – after their defeat – *freedom fighters*. The events of October were first called *revolt*, then *rising* (in Ireland only) and, again posthumously, *revolution*. Those who participated in the events had never any doubts that they were fighting for freedom, and for that the vehicle was *revolution*. But as the revolution was repressed by Russian arms, the oppressors invented their own vocabulary to describe it. In 1957 it was called *counter-revolution*, by the Kádár regime until the mid 1980s. In the last five years of the Soviet imperium it was referred to as *the regretful events* of 1956, while in late 1988, early 1989 it was renamed *uprising*. The name *revolution* reappeared in June 1989, with the severing of the Soviet political bond.

Foreign reporting of the revolution, from 25 October onwards, had relied on a variety of sources: MTI, Reuters, BBC, journalists in Vienna, eyewitnesses, Hungarian radio broadcasts, Radio Free Europe in Munich. and small pirate radio stations, broadcasting from various localities in Budapest, and in larger towns in the country. In terms of Irish reporting many news items and comments came via the diplomatic correspondent of the *Irish Times*, relying on unspecified sources.

In the morning of 25 October something unprecedented in Hungarian history and spine-chilling in execution occurred in Parliament square, Budapest. A peaceful crowd of several thousand demonstrators, with a friendly and beflagged Russian T34 tank leading their column, was approaching the parliament building. Delegates from the crowd were to hand in a petition to the government

4 From the largest Soviet army camp near Kecskemét, about 70 miles from Budapest.

requesting the withdrawal of Soviet forces. The square was guarded by other, not friendly Russian tanks and, on the opposite side, on the roofs of tall buildings, unbeknown to the demonstrators, the state security police had taken up positions. Shortly before 11 a.m. they opened fire on the unarmed crowd below. In the massacre that followed some six hundred people were slaughtered, the friendly Soviet tank was captured by the other tanks, the bodies of the butchered demonstrators were either pushed into the Danube, or carried away in lorries.

Reporting to the university newspaper as a student journalist, I photographed six dead bodies at one single spot of six square yards around a statue.

The event was variously reported in the world press, some witnessing of the wounded being treated in overcrowded hospitals. The exact number of casualties has never been established, nor have the perpetrators been punished to the present day. However, the massacre led to a series of indirect results. Fighting flared up again in earnest, between the insurgents on one side, the state police and the Soviets on the other; tanks were immobilised by petrol bombs, the workers gathered in factories and formed a Free Trade Union, the revolutionaries' army council distributed leaflets that said: 'We swear by the corpses of our martyrs we shall win freedom' (*Irish Times*, 27 October, front page). Amnesties for arms handed in were announced by Budapest Radio, while in New York the United Nations began to discuss the motion whether the presence of Russian troops in Hungary was, or was not legitimate. President Eisenhower deplored the Soviet intervention but offered nothing else except sympathy for the Hungarians. (American food parcels and medicine reached Hungary later.)

After the weekend the Monday morning papers were full with Hungarian reports, comments and pictures and (*Irish Times*, 29 October, front page) even maps. Imre Nagy, made hastily prime minister once again after the popular demand, seemed to be in command of the situation in the weekend; he announced the withdrawal of the Soviet troops (*Irish Times*, 29 October) and ordered the ceasefire of the government troops, which were, at that time, divided into pro-revolutionary and neutral troops. Only the secret police had active fighting units; the street police had either been neutral, or had handed over their arms to the revolutionaries.

The Security Council of the UN deliberated again on the Hungarian situation, and again in vain. Shepilov, the Soviet foreign secretary, stated that the Soviet troops would leave Budapest if the rebels lay down their arms (*Irish Times*, 30 October). Alas, on the same, the penultimate day of October, some disturbing global news were also reported by the same paper. Israeli troops drove into Egypt during the previous day. This was to be the first sign of the Suez war, later involving the French and the English, which was regarded by the Soviets as a convenient diversion and a clear opportunity to finish off Hungary. With laudable perspicacity and foresight the editorial in 27 October of the *Irish Independent*, entitled: 'Hungary and the Czars', drew a comparison between the 1849 and the 1956 Russian invasion of Hungary.

Initially, on 29 and 30 October Soviet troops did move out of the city of Budapest (*Irish Independent*, 30, 31 October) but no further than the edges of the outlying districts, where the tanks were placed, or dug in in defensive positions (*Irish Times*, 30, 31 October, 1 November). Western commentators in general, Irish and English journalists in particular, were reluctant to forecast events in Hungary, although they faithfully reported changes: in the government, in the symbols of the nation's flag, in the attitudes to one party rule and to free elections. The reformed Nagy government was now composed of Communists (their new leader was János Kádár), Social Democrats, Smallholders, and others. The new defence minister, Pál Maléter,[5] recently colonel of an armoured division of the Hungarian army which sided with the revolutionaries, more or less united the fighting units of Budapest. The first phase of the armed struggle, which started in the evening of 23 October was over by the 29th. Despite the heavy casualties, the fire at the National Museum, the wreck and ruin of the radio building and other edifices, the barricades that had rendered many roads impassable, there was a feeling of quiet jubilation in the capital, and all over the country, where secret policemen were captured, communist officials had been chased away and new leaders were elected. All this proved to be a pyrrhic victory.

The prime minister promised free elections on 30 October (*Irish Times*, 31 October) On November 1, All Saints day, every window in Budapest had a lit candle; the cardinal, József Mindszenty, freed the day before, gave a conciliatory, yet uncompromising speech on Hungarian radio. On the same day, Cardinal D'Alton, 'in the name of Catholic Ireland', sent a message to Mindszenty, greatly rejoicing in the release of his Hungarian colleague (*Irish Independent*, 2 November).

A 'soldier's council' had been formed (*Irish Times*, 1 November) for the protection of the population. In truth this was the new National Guard, made up of former street police, soldiers and freedom fighters on 30 October, and still recruiting new members on 2 and 3 November. My name was registered as Guard 06332 on 31 October. The secret police had been officially disbanded on 29 October, but two days later a group of them were still holding out defending the besieged Communist Party headquarters on Republic square. They were caught by the crowd and twelve of them were lynched in the afternoon of 31 October.

The unsettling news on 2 November seemed to have reached the foreign press (front-page reports, *Irish Independent*, *Irish Times*) before they reached the people on the streets of Budapest. The government was, of course, informed of new Russian tanks crossing Hungary's eastern borders, and of a 'ring of steel around

5 On 3 November Maléter was lured to the Russian Headquarters in Cscpel island for 'negotiations'. It was a trap. He was arrested, then executed.

the capital' formed by tanks that had moved out of the city. Nagy announced Hungary's withdrawal from the Warsaw Pact (*Irish Times*, 2 November, front-page report) and appealed to the United Nations 'to consider the position of Hungary at the earliest opportunity' (ibid.). On 3 November (*Irish Times*, *Irish Independent*, front-page reports) the Russians kept advancing towards the capital, while other units as good as sealed the Hungarian-Austrian frontier at the West.

The second, and totally devastating Soviet attack came at the early hours of the morning on Sunday, 4 November 1956. Divisions of the Hungarian army (lead by General Béla Király), parts of the National Guard, and fighting groups of independent insurgents put up a hand-to-hand, building-to-building fight for a week, at great cost to Hungarian life and with a widespread destruction of buildings. Bombed in 1944-5, Budapest once more was half-destroyed. 'A Hungarian reporter looked out on the battle of Budapest yesterday and tapped out his story on the teleprinter' – which the *Irish Independent* reproduced on 6 November.

The week's fighting was continuously reported in the *Irish Times*, and the *Irish Independent*, (5-10 November) relying on such sources as Radio Budapest, Radio Moscow, Radio Free Europe, and Reuters. As soon as the tanks once again reached Parliament square, and the radio building, in another district it was announced that a new government had been formed under the premiership of János Kádár, and that the '*conspiracy*', led by the previous government, had been crushed.

Imre Nagy's dramatic last cry 'Help Hungary' was transmitted by Budapest Radio in the early hours of the morning of 4 November 1956. Recorded and transmitted by the BBC it reverberated through radio stations of Europe, from Dublin to Rome, Stockholm, Oslo. Nagy and his entourage later sought refuge in the Yugoslav embassy whence they were eventually hounded out, arrested and transferred to a secret location in Romania. Previous to that, 'Moscow puppet premier János Kádár met Imre Nagy ... in a desperate attempt to gain popular support' (*Irish Independent*, 12 November) but Nagy, then still in the Yugoslav embassy, refused to give in to the Soviets (*Irish Independent*, 15 November). After his arrest Nagy's fate was sealed: he and his closest associates were executed in June 1958, by which time all other revolutionary fighters and participants had been rounded up. It is estimated that around four hundred people were also executed (some, who were under age, not until they reached their eighteenth year), and many thousands were jailed, their sentences running from one year to life imprisonment. Among friends and acquaintances of mine: G. Endre (tram driver) and I. Hegedüs (pentathlon athlete) killed in the fighting; T. Déry (novelist of world renown), I. Eörsi (then journalist, now playwright), Á. Göncz (then secretary to Nagy, now president of the Republic of Hungary) and G. Krassó (political activist), each sentenced for seven years' imprisonment.

Pocket resistance in Csepel island, and in various other parts of the country Mecsek-Pécs; Vác; the environs of Miskolc; a 'movable spot' at the Balaton region; and a border post on the Austrian frontier was still being reported: *Irish Times*, 8 November, 13 November, *Irish Independent*, 10 November), and 'private', that is uncaptured, free radio stations operated on Hungarian territory until the very end of November. With the main military operations over, two other crises gripped the capital; the wounded had taken all the hospital beds, and camp-beds in makeshift clinics too, but there wasn't enough medicine and blood to sustain them; while those physically unharmed refused to go back to work, so a general workers' strike paralysed all Hungary, right through November. Sporadic strikes continued in December (*Irish Times*, 12, 14 December), some involving violent clashes between the pickets and the police.

Those who had engaged in revolutionary activities, and managed to avoid capture, hid outside the capital, or crossed the frontiers to Austria or to Yugoslavia. Both the Irish *Times* and the *Irish Independent* of 6 November speak of the revulsion the Western world felt, and expressed, at the second Russian attack. The *Irish Times* (9 November) gives an account of Irish students demonstrating at Trinity College Dublin, and of an intrusion by Irish students into the premises of 'New Books', a Soviet-sympathiser organisation. On the same day Trinity students handed in a petition, pleading for the cause of Hungary, to the American embassy. In the North, students at Queen's University, Belfast, held a hugh protest meeting and later marched into Belfast centre at night to protest at the premises of a Communist-oriented bookshop (they were dispersed by police). The Irish branch of the International Federation of Transport Workers asked the government on 12 November (*Irish Times*, *Irish Independent*) to support proposals 'leading to the resurrection of Hungary'.

One can readily see that Griffith's words reverberated in Irish hearts and minds. And one can also surmise, from other responses (such as Desmond Fennell's article from Vienna, *Irish Times*, 13 November) that 1956 was associated with another revolution that had taken place forty years earlier in Ireland.

Pope Pius XII., a champion of anti-communism all his life, issued an encyclical on Hungary on 6 November 1956, which was being read on 11 November in Catholic churches in Ireland, and in the rest of the free world. He said: 'The blood of the Hungarian people cries to the Lord' (*Irish Independent*, 6 November).

There was yet another type of aggression, the news of which reached Irish eyes and ears on 14 November 1956 (RTE evening news bulletin; *Irish Times*, front page) The previous day, Hungarian railway workers in the east of the country stopped a train by blowing up a railway line, and freed a train-load of prisoners from being deported to Russia.

Out of the many comments, analyses and laments I would like to sum up the articles of Desmond Fennell (*Irish Times*, 8 and 13 November), Russell Jones

(*Irish Times*, 15 and 20 December), Barrett McGurk (*Irish Independent*, 8 and 26 November) and the speech of Josip Broz Tito, president of Yugoslavia (*Irish Times* report, 16 November, front page). Fennell's first report came from Nickelsdorf, a frontier post still in Hungarian hands. He witnessed the crossing of unarmed Hungarian soldiers as refugees into Austria, followed by many civilian refugees, and reported on the general disillusionment they all felt about the West that had failed to help Hungary. Reporting from Vienna, Fennell described the visit he had paid to Traisdorf refugee camp, on 12 November, witnessing the distribution of clothing and food by the Red Cross. He had interviewed young Hungarian refugee workers who were keen to find employment in the West, and encountered one hundred and eighty students, and staff from Sopron University. Later in the year the entire faculty of forestry and wood engineering of that university escaped to Austria, and in 1957 transferred to Vancouver, in Canada.

Russell Jones, of United Press, in his first article (*Irish Times*, 15 December) analysed the background to the Hungarian revolution: the privileges of its elite classes, the bitter harvest of the oppression of the people, the dashed hopes of Hungarians who had trusted the West. He also touched on topical events: Cardinal Mindszenty's refuge at the American embassy, the disappearance of the prime minister, Imre Nagy, and the penetration of the revolution to all towns and rural communities in Hungary. His second article was entitled: 'Kremlin loses claim to represent poor' (*Irish Times*, 20 December). This piece of pungent writing exposed the hypocrisy of Nikita Kruschev's claims to 'portray the Hungarian uprising as the work of capitalists and fascists'. In Jones' view the Soviet Union was an imperialist power which did not represent the poor. He concluded his article on an optimistic note: 'Against all logic and reason I want to believe that the Hungarians, who have written in blood their faith in all good and decent things in life, will not fail.'

But for the immediate post-revolutionary time let me recall the words of an inscription on the damaged gable of a ruined apartment block in Budapest: 'Workers rejoice, Big Brother is back.'

McGurk, an Irish-American journalist reporting from Vienna, described a growing refugee crisis in the Austrian capital, calling it the exodus of the bitter fruits of the Hungarian uprising, and referring to the refugees as 'Hungary walks weeping on icy roads to the West'.

Marshall Tito, we may remember, was a communist leader himself, who had once quarrelled with Stalin, was reconciled to Kruschev, and gave temporary asylum to Nagy and his closest associates and, eventually, to three thousand Hungarian refugees in 1956. His speech on 15 November criticised the Stalinist methods of Hungary's despots and their henchmen, and believed that the rising of the Hungarians was justified. Later, under Soviet pressure, he was to qualify his remarks.

The second aspect of our investigation relates to the inaction of the United Nations during the Hungarian crisis, and to the brave role Irish representatives played at various UN sessions in New York. Much smaller, and a good deal weaker than today, the UN had an indecisive general secretary, in the person of Dag Hammerskjöld, who hesitated even at times when no risks were involved.

The first appeal to the UN was sent by the beleaguered prime minister, Imre Nagy, on 1 November 1956: 'To consider the position of Hungary at the earliest possible moment' (*Irish Times*, 2 November 1956). This was of no avail. Although the general assembly, as well as the security council of the UN, discussed the Hungarian question something like twelve times between the end of October and the end of December, the international body was either paralysed by vetoes of the Soviet Union, or it was in mortal fear of acting decisively lest it should spark off a chain of events that may lead to a world war. In the 16 November *Irish Times* a Vatican commentator was quoted, saying: 'The free world, frightened by Russian war threats, had left Hungary alone in its struggle for freedom' (front page). The fear echoed through sections of Western society, including individuals in Ireland. For instance, Mr E. Blythe, managing director of the Abbey Theatre, stated at the debate held by UCD Cuman Gaeleach on 20 November: 'It would be wrong for the West to take military action on behalf of Hungary' (*Irish Independent*, 21 November).

At the tail end of the first Russian attack, on 29 October 1956, Sean McBride TD sent a telegram of good wishes and sympathy to the then free government of Imre Nagy, which was reciprocated with thanks by the Hungarian minister in Paris, Pál Auer (*Irish Times*, 31 October). This Irish welcome to free Hungary turned into a strong concern, during the second phase of the Russian attack, when Liam Cosgrave, minister for foreign affairs, attended the UN general session on 7 November and insisted on a general debate on Hungary (*Irish Times*, 8 November, front page, and RTE Sound Archives recording). This gallant gesture was followed by another one, three weeks later. On 30 November Cosgrave accused the Soviet Union in the UN general assembly for being 'the legitimate heir to old imperialism', and stated that 'Hungary was a victim of colonialism' (*Irish Times*, 1 December, front page). Irish delegate F.H. Boland's voice could also be heard previously by the assembly, on 8 November: 'We are profoundly confident that the Hungarian nation, which has won the respect of the world, will arise again.' It did arise, peacefully, thirty-three years later.

Vatican Radio added its voice to the UN debate declaring, that the UN had an undeniable duty to take action in Hungary. Well, a vote was taken on 9 November: 'UN general assembly in New York called on Russia to withdraw her troops from Hungary. By 48 votes to 11, with 16 abstentions, the assembly voted for a resolution introduced by Italy, and co-sponsored by Ireland, Pakistan, Cuba and Peru.'

Although subsequent UN debates were ineffective, or blocked, or brought no pro-active decisions, the puppet Kádár government did allow medicine, food and clothing to reach Hungary, either through the UN or directly from aid agencies. On the other hand, they had repeatedly refused to allow a UN delegation to enter Hungary and investigate the disappearance of many thousand of Hungarians allegedly transported to Russia. (The UN debate of 13 November was reported next day in the *Irish Independent*.) When, at long last, the Kádár government's initial objections turned to indifference, Hammerskjöld declined to make a visit (*Irish Times*, 6 December 1956).

Meanwhile the Irish had been taking their fair share in collecting money for food, and supplying blood plasma. On 16 November (*Irish Times, Irish Independent*) Dr J. P. O'Riordan reported that the supplies of blood plasma had reached their destination. The first consignment of Irish food had already reached Vienna on 2 November 1956 – a very speedy action, under the circumstances.

Let us end this section with the precis of an Irish delegate to the UN, Conor Cruise O'Brien. On 8 December he told the political committee of the UN in New York that 'It had failed to cope with Russian aggression in Hungary' (*Irish Times*, 9 December).

On 22 December the *Irish Times* reproduced a faithful translation of a poem by Sándor Petöfi, written in 1849 but perfectly befitting the situation in 1956. It is entitled: 'Europe is silent.' Here is the opening stanza:

> Europe is silent, silent again
> Its revolutions have blown over …
> Shame on it! It quietened down
> Without winning its freedom.

In highlighting the Irish effort on behalf of the Hungarian refugees one must praise the swift efficiency of the Irish branch of the Red Cross. But, as we shall see, others joined in with helping hands, first with the collection of money, food, medicine, then with the welcome of the refugees: churches, organisations, cities, villages and individual families. Even though I am not here to map up the full Irish effort, I wish to give enough representative examples to show that – indeed – a small nation's heart went out to comfort another small nation's sons and daughters, in their misery.

I would like to refer to the Dáil debate on 7 November when Mr Cosgrave said that the world had heard with horror of the renewed treacherous onslaught by the Soviet military machine on Hungary. This was followed by a private notice question, recorded as 'Relief for Hungary'. I am quoting the record in *Dáil Éireann, Parliamentary Debates*, 7 November 1956:

Mr de Valera: I gave private notice that I intended asking the Taoiseach whether the Government proposed to make any special contribution to the funds of the Irish Red Cross to enable it to play its part in relieving suffering in Hungary and in assisting the Hungarian refugees.

The Taoiseach: The Irish Red Cross Society, out of the funds already available to them, have sent certain consignments to Austria for the relief of the people of Hungary and are in course of sending further consignments of clothing, food and medical supplies.

As was announced last night the society has launched a national appeal for funds to help Hungary, and a national collection for the purpose will be made throughout the country next Sunday.

The Deputy, the House and the country may rest assured that, to such extent as the Society's funds in hands, as supplemented by the proceeds of the national appeal and by the generous contributions in kind that the Society is receiving from our people, may prove insufficient, the Government will readily take steps to place the Society in funds to provide relief for the victims of the aggression in Hungary.

The part that it may be practicable for us to take in assisting the Hungarian refugees is being considered in consultation with the Irish Red Cross Society.

The Minister for External Affairs has already, this afternoon, given expression, in this House, to our feelings of sympathy with the people of Poland and Hungary, of admiration for the matchless courage they have displayed in their unequal struggle for freedom and human rights and of abhorrence of the ruthless measures of suppression to which the people of Hungary have been subjected. I have no doubt whatever that, by a generous response to the appeal of the Irish Red Cross Society, our people will show their practical sympathy with the Hungarian people in a manner more striking and effective than any action that it would be within the Government's power to take.

Mr de Valera: While agreeing with that, the only question is time. Are there sufficient reserves to enable them to act quickly?

The Taoiseach: Yes.

Following the Red Cross's swift actions, mentioned above, it was the Catholic Church's turn on 8 November, when 'The Archbishop of Dublin, the Most Reverend Dr McQuaid, announced that a collection will be made in all the churches of the Diocese of Dublin on November 18th for the victims of the atrocities' (*Irish Times*, 9 November). This was followed by the lord mayor of

Dublin's call for a civic collection for the 'Children of Hungary' (*Irish Times*, 9 November). By 12 November it had been decided that Ireland would take refugees from Hungary. The offers for help now poured in from many quarters: the Irish Countrywomen's Association, the Irish Branch of the Institute of Catholic Girl's Society (*Irish Times*, 12 November) and individual Dublin families. The latter had rapidly collected £1000. From the proceeds of a grand variety show in Dublin on 25 November, another sum reached the coffers, and yet another church collection on the same date yielded further thousands (*Irish Independent*, 16, 17 November). An undeclared sum was also transferred to the Relief Fund from the proceeds of an exhibition table tennis match by the Hungarian national team (*Irish Independent*, 10 December). Let us remember, that we have to multiply all 1956 sums by thirty to get today's values.

On 25 November the first group of Hungarian refugees arrived at Shannon airport and were welcomed by the mayor. Earlier, Mr Tadhg O'Sullivan, a member of the Irish legation in Switzerland, travelled to Vienna to give the refugees Irish identity papers. 'We are glad to be in a Christian country,' one of them was reported saying (*Irish Independent*, 26 November).

The first hundred and eighty Hungarians were followed by two more groups in 1956, so by the end of the year five hundred and thirty Hungarians, all transported by Aer Lingus, were here to stay (*Irish Independent*, 8 December), some for good, some for a good while. The original target of one thousand persons was never reached, mainly because other alternatives were to open up for placing Hungarian refugees at other parts of the world. The Hungarian exodus in 1956-7 (the borders were tightly sealed after April) totalled approximately one hundred and eighty thousand people,[6] about 2 per cent of the population of Hungary at the time. In the course of 1957-8 about one quarter of the refugees (mainly agricultural workers and their families) returned to Hungary. Nine persons returned from Ireland.

There was space for five hundred refugees in Knockalinsheen, a former army camp, County Clare, near Limerick, where the Hungarians were housed. The first family to be individually helped by an Irish sponsor, Mr Walter Smithwick, was a lawyer and his wife (*Irish Independent*, 27 November). With Red Cross help many refugees in Ireland settled in well enough (*Irish Times*, *Irish Independent*, 27, 28 November) and the collection on their behalf increased by £3,700 from the Irish Save the Children Fund, and by £17,000 from the Presbyterian Church collection. Donations came from the North too, and some Hungarian families were eventually migrated up there, although Northern Ireland had no refugee policy. The target for the Irish collections was £80,000. 'It has been estimated by

---

6 The United States took over fifty thousand, Canada about thirty thousand, Britain twenty thousand refugees.

Mr Sean Ó Morain, assistant secretary of the Department of Defence, and treasurer of the Irish Red Cross Society, that £80,000 would be needed to provide for the refugees for one year' (*Irish Times*, 4 December). This was judged to be enough time for them to find housing and employment, in other words, to integrate into Irish society.

At length, by the end of 1956 the target sum exceeded £104,000 (*Irish Times*, 27 December). By mid-December Shannon airport was becoming a busy junction for many more plane-loads of Hungarians wishing to settle in the United States and in Canada. One of them, Béla Szabó, a young boy of thirteen, made the headlines in the *Irish Times*, and in the *Irish Independent*, 14 December. With his group of freedom fighters he had knocked out Russian tanks with petrol bombs, later to be named 'Molotov cocktails' by Western journalists. Béla Szabó was presented with a real/symbolic Christmas tree at the airport.

The general situation was varied; then camp conditions deteriorated in January 1957 when refugees complained of leaking roofs, damp conditions, and lack of work. Somehow this reflected the general situation in Ireland at the time (*Irish Times*, 15 August, 1992). Yet, when we put everything in the balance, the refugees did not fare badly, and some – like my friends. the Letoha and the Polgár families – integrated well, and looked forward to a rewarding life in Ireland. Looking back to the tail end of the year 1956, from a distance of forty-three years, one can say that out of the Knockalinsheen entrants about one hundred families/single persons, with eventual Irish spouses, have made their home in Ireland, and I am glad to see some of them and their descendants in this audience.

Thirteen years ago, when we were celebrating the thirtieth anniversary of the Hungarian revolution, Mr J. and Mrs G. Polgár were interviewed by Eanna Brophy: 'The night they fled Hungary's red terror' (*Irish Independent*, 23 October 1986), and I spoke to a reporter of RTE in Maynooth. His last question was: 'How long would communism last in your view?' I replied: 'A very long time.' Within three years communism was collapsing everywhere. Unlike other false prophets in history I am very happy to have been proved wrong.[7]

---

7 Suggestions for further reading:

Federigo Argentieri, *Ungheria, 1956*, 2nd ed. (Milan, 1998)

Alan Blackwood, *The Hungarian uprising* (Hove, 1996)

British Report to the UN Special Committee on Hungary, 21 February 1957. PRO FO 371.128672. NH. 10110/194

Terry Cox, *Reconsidering the Hungarian revolution of 1956* (London and Portland, 1997)

Dáil Éireann, *Parliamentary debates*, 7 November, 1956; private notice question, 'Relief for Hungary'

Péter Gosztonyi, 'Der Volkaufstand in Ungarn, 1956', *Aus Politik und Zeitgeschichte*, 1996, pp. 3-14

'Hungarian diary, October-November 1956', selected radio broadcasts, RTE Sound Library and Archives

Hungary's revolutions: the catalogue of an exhibition, commemorating the 25th anniversary of the
     1956 Revolution, compiled by Thomas Kabdebo (Manchester, 1981)
Irish Independent, 22 October – 31 December 1956
Irish Times, 22 October – 31 December 1956
Thomas Kabdebo, *A time for everything*, translated by Len Rix (Maynooth, 1996)
Budapest 1956-1996 ... réd. et présentation de François Fejtö et Gilles Martinet (Paris, 1997)
Melvin J. Lasky (ed.), *The Hungarian Revolution* (London, 1957)
Anna Letoha (an interview with Mrs Anna Letoha) RTE broadcast, 23 October 1986
Bill Lomax, *Hungary, 1956* (London, 1976)
Angela Long, 'First crack in the communist system', *Irish Times*, 28 October 1996
George Mikes, *A study in infamy: the operations of the Hungarian secret police* (London, 1958)
Heino Nyyssönen, 'Revolution, Uprising Counter-Revolution, naming the events of 1956 in
     Hungary'. A lecture delivered at the 26th World Congress of the International Political Science
     Association, Berlin, 1994.
Aidan O'Connor (compiler): 'The Hungarian revolution, October – November 1956' (Dublin,
     1996). A folder of unpublished notes and published newspaper writings, constituting a diary of
     events.
'Unliberated Europe'. *Twentieth Century*, vol. 162, no. 966 (1957).

PART TWO

7

Arthur Griffith and his times: a bibliography

Thomas Kabdebo and Brian Maye

Introduction

Jacqueline Hill

Arthur Griffith (1872-1922) was one of the most influential Irish nationalists of his generation. Born in Dublin, educated by the Christian Brothers, and a printer by trade, as a young man he was linked with several societies and clubs that represented an advanced nationalist position, including the Irish Republican Brotherhood and the Gaelic League. He was also a supporter of the charismatic leader of the Irish parliamentary party, Charles Stewart Parnell. Early on Griffith displayed a flair for journalism, and it was through journalism that he was to make his chief impact on nationalists in Ireland and elsewhere. Two aspects of Griffith's ideas were particularly significant. First, influenced by continental writers such as the German economist Friedrich List, he argued that national independence must be reinforced not only by cultural but by economic independence. Ireland should have the power to develop her own industries behind tariff barriers. This ran counter to the prevailing 'free trade' ethos of the United Kingdom. Secondly, in response to the stalling in the 1890s of the home rule campaign – the leader of the Liberal party in Britain, W.E. Gladstone, had failed to keep the party united behind his home rule policy, while the Irish parliamentary party had been bedevilled by splits since the Parnell divorce case – Griffith offered a simple solution. Irish parliamentary representation was predominantly nationalist, so withdrawal from Westminster would return the centre of political gravity to Ireland. There existed a notional Irish precedent, in the form of Daniel O'Connell's putative 'Council of Three Hundred' in the 1840s; moreover, from his somewhat idiosyncratic reading of Austrian history Griffith was convinced that a withdrawal from the imperial diet by the Hungarians in 1861 had played a key part in the establishment of a Hungarian assembly, leading to the Austrian-Hungarian *Ausgleich* of 1867. These were among the ideas he expounded in his newspaper, the *United Irishman* (1899-1906), and in *The Resurrection of Hungary: a Parallel to Ireland* (1904). Such a programme posed a challenge both to the Irish parliamentary party and to the various separatist groups.

As his interest in the Austro-Hungarian dual monarchy showed, Griffith, though temperamentally a separatist, was pragmatic in respect of forms of self-government; indeed, he was an admirer of the 'kingdom of Ireland', and the 'constitution of 1782', which he assumed (wrongly) had conveyed executive as well as legislative powers to the pre-union Irish parliament. At all events, by 1902 he was urging what became known as his 'Hungarian policy' on Irish MPs: that they should remain at home, taking on the powers of a *de facto* Irish government. Thus British rule in Ireland would be rendered impotent by a species of 'passive resistance'. This visionary programme was to be a key policy of Sinn Féin ('We Ourselves'), founded in 1905 at a convention in Dublin at which Griffith expounded his views to a variety of (mostly separatist) nationalists.

Between 1905 and 1914 the organisation made only modest progress, but Griffith continued to communicate through his newspaper, *Sinn Féin* (1906-14). He was critical of the government's proposed home rule bill of 1912 for its failure to grant effective control over revenues. When World War One broke out in 1914 Griffith was among those (mostly IRB members) who discussed an armed uprising – he was as pragmatic about the means as about the form of independence. He was named a member of the proposed civil government, but was apparently not in the inner councils of those who planned the details of the Easter Rising of 1916. This was ironic in view of the almost immediate tendency for the Rising to be designated the 'Sinn Féin rebellion'. This description brought the organisation into the public eye, and Griffith was temporarily imprisoned, and his newspaper suppressed. More Sinn Féin clubs were established, and there were some by-election victories. At this point in the evolution of Sinn Féin policy the form of the future government of Ireland – whether monarchical or republican – was still not settled.

The conscription crisis of 1918 brought together representatives of various nationalist bodies in opposition to the government's proposal to extend conscription to Ireland. Several Sinn Féin leaders, including Griffith, were arrested on the pretext that they were collaborating with Germany. Griffith decided to contest a by-election in East Cavan; his plight as a prisoner reinforced his appeal and won him a resounding victory. At the general election (December 1918) that followed the ending of the war, Sinn Féin candidates secured 73 of the 105 Irish seats; the once impregnable parliamentary party won only six seats. The opportunity now arose of putting Griffith's 'Hungarian policy' into practice. In January 1919 those Sinn Féin MPs who were not in prison assembled in Dublin as the first Dáil Éireann ('Irish parliament') and established a provisional government. Griffith, who some years earlier had yielded the presidency of Sinn Féin to Eamon de Valera, was named minister for home affairs, and for a time was acting president; in the second dáil (1921) he was minister for foreign affairs.

Towards the end of the war of independence (1919-21) Griffith was made leader of the five delegates appointed to negotiate an agreement with Lloyd George's government. He regarded the terms on offer from the British – dominion status, with the power of control over economic and fiscal policy – acceptable, and he was therefore prepared to sign the Anglo-Irish treaty (December 1921). Despite opposition from de Valera and others, a majority of the Dáil accepted the treaty in January 1922, and Griffith was elected president of Dáil Éireann in place of de Valera. He died suddenly, of a brain haemorrhage, in August 1922.

Although he impressed Lloyd George by his negotiating skills, Arthur Griffith was primarily a man of ideas and a writer rather than an orator or administrator. At a time of great ideological ferment he exercised enormous influence, as the many tributes to him on his untimely death testified.

Bibliography

This attempt at a bibliography is justified, simply, by being more complete than other previous ones. It brings together the bibliographic aspect of Brian Maye's research, most of which can be found in his book, *Arthur Griffith* (Dublin, 1997), and of Thomas Kabdebo's research, *The Hungarian-Irish 'Parallel' and Arthur Griffith's use of his sources* (Maynooth, 1988), and his scan of all the newspapers and journals Griffith contributed to.

Part I lists *works by Arthur Griffith*, with a standard bibliographic description. *Items without page numbers have been located only in a catalogue.*

Part II lists *works about Arthur Griffith*, with as much detail as Part I.

Part III presents titles under the heading of '*Arthur Griffith and his times*' with the normal basic scholarly references. Notes added to certain entries indicate the location of an item in a given library.

LIBRARIES AND ARCHIVES

Libraries
The principal depositories of printed Griffith sources:
British Library
Library of Congress, Washington
National Library of Ireland, Dublin
National University of Ireland, Maynooth and the Library of St Patrick's College, Maynooth
Trinity College Dublin Library
University College Cork Library, now NUI, Cork.

Archives
National Library of Ireland: Barton Papers; Griffith Papers; Holloway Diary; Labour Pamphlet Collection; Lennon Papers; McGarrity Papers, O'Kelly Papers; O'Luing Papers, Documents relating to Arthur Griffith, UCD Library

Saint Patrick's College, Maynooth: 'Griffith Archives' (copies of correspondence
    from other Dublin archives and research relating to 'Hungarian Affinities') and
    other relevant documents
Trinity College Dublin: Arthur Griffith correspondence; Erskine Childers
    correspondence

ABBREVIATIONS

Bibliog	Bibliography	NUIM	National University of Ireland, Maynooth
BL	British Library		
facs.	Facsimile	PM	Prime Minister
FO	Foreign Office	PRO	Public Record Office
illus.	illustration(s)	SPM	St Patrick's College Maynooth
Köt	Kötet (volume)	TCD	Trinity College, University of Dublin
LC	Library of Congress		
MP	Member of Parliament	UCC	University College Cork, now NUI, Cork
NLI	National Library of Ireland		
		UCD	University College Dublin

WORKS BY ARTHUR GRIFFITH

Books and articles written by Arthur Griffith

Griffith, Arthur. 'A ballad history of Ireland'. (An album of clippings from the
    United Irishman.) Dublin, 1904. Signed: *Cuguan.* SPM. (Published in parts
    between 2 January 1904 and 2 December 1905.)
Griffith, Arthur. 'A pot of broth'. *United Irishman*, 8 November 1902, p. 3.
    Signed: *Cuguan.*
Griffith, Arthur. *Address to the representatives of foreign nations, adopted at the
    January seminar of Dáil Éireann, 1921*. Dublin: Dáil Éireann, 1921. NLI.
Griffith, Arthur. *A new position: Republican leaders' efforts to end the struggle.*
    Dublin: Sinn Féin, 1908. 4pp. NLI.
Griffith, Arthur. *Arguments for the Treaty.* Dublin: Martin Lester, 1922. 32pp.
    NLI. SPM (Pamphlets vol. 1817).
Griffith, Arthur. *Arthur Griffith to David Lloyd George.* (Facsimiles of letters, 13
    December 1921.) 2pp. NLI, SPM/NUIM.
Griffith, Arthur. 'British Government and Irish Trade'. *Nationality*, 31 July
    1915, p. 1.
Griffith, Arthur. *Cumann na nGaedheal.* (A circular asking to approve British
    recruitment in Ireland for the Boer War.) Dublin, 1902. 1 p. NLI.

Griffith, Arthur. (Cumann na nGaedheal 'amendment' of 1902). *United Irishman*, 1 November 1902, p. 3. NLI. SPM/NUIM.

Griffith, Arthur. Dáil Éireann, 19 December, 1921, motion by Arthur Griffith: 'That Dáil Éireann approves of the Treaty between Great Britain and Ireland signed in London on 5 December, 1912.' In *Debate on the Treaty of Iris Dháil Éireann*, Dublin: Talbot Press, 1922, p. 20.

Griffith, Arthur. *Dublin Castle exhumed – Redmond, Devlin, Dillon.* Dublin: Whelan, 1916.

Griffith, Arthur. *Economic salvation and the means to attain it; selected and arranged by Seamus Whelan.* Dublin: Whelan, 1911. 6pp. NLI, UCC, SPM (photocopy in Griffith archives).

Griffith, Arthur. *England's colossal robbery of Ireland. The final relations of the two countries since the Union.* (Extracts from Griffith's speech on 22 October 1906.) Dublin: Sinn Féin National Council, 1906. 2pp.

Griffith, Arthur. 'Home rule and government'. *United Irishman*, 8 November 1902, p. 3.

Griffith, Arthur. *How Ireland has 'prospered' under English rule and the slave mind.* New York: Irish Progressive League, 1900.

Griffith, Arthur. *How Ireland is taxed: an address delivered before the Central Branch of the National Council, September, 1916.* Dublin: Duffy, 1907. National Council Pamphlets, 6. 5pp. LC, NLI.

Griffith, Arthur. 'Important letter of 1919', reprinted in *Capuchin Annual*, 1969, pp. 330–5.

Griffith, Arthur. 'In the Dublin Mountains'. *United Irishman*, 30 August 1902, p. 3. Signed: *Cuguan*.

Griffith, Arthur. 'Ireland and English literature'. *United Irishman*, 5 April 1902, p. 3. Signed: *Cuguan*.

Griffith, Arthur. 'Ireland and Spain and an English slander'. *United Irishman*, 14 February 1903, p. 6.

Griffith, Arthur. *Ireland's economic situation: England's Irish philanthropy.* Washington: Friends of Irish Freedom, 1920; reprint by National Bureau of Information, 1921. 7pp.

Griffith, Arthur. 'Irish prose literature'. *United Irishman*, 27 September 1902, p. 3. Signed: *Cuguan*.

Griffith, Arthur. 'John F. Taylor'. *United Irishman*, 15 November 1902, p. 3. Signed: *Cuguan*.

Griffith, Arthur. 'King Arthur an Irishman?' *United Irishman*, 20 December 1902, p. 5. Signed: *Cuguan*.

Griffith, Arthur. 'Kuno Meyer on Ancient Ireland'. *United Irishman*, 10 May 1903, p. 6. Signed: *Cuguan*.

Griffith, Arthur. 'Language and other things'. *United Irishman*, 15 March 1902, p. 3.

Griffith, Arthur. 'Language, literature and nationality'. *United Irishman*, 11 March 1902, p. 3. Signed: *Cuguan*.

Griffith, Arthur. 'Lionel Johnson's Work'. *United Irishman*, 18 October 1902, p. 3. Signed: *Cuguan*.

Griffith, Arthur. *Michael Collins: Commemorative Booklet*. Dublin, n.d.

Griffith, Arthur. 'Mitchel and Irish Literature'. *United Irishman*, 7 June 1903, p. 3. Signed: *Cuguan*.

Griffith, Arthur. 'Petofi, poet and patriot'. *United Irishman*, 24 December 1904, pp. 2-3. Signed: *Carganac*. (Attributed to Arthur Griffith.)

Griffith, Arthur (preface by) in Lillian M. Fogarty: *James Fintan Lalor, patriot and political essayist, 1807-1849*. Dublin, Talbot Press; London: T. Fisher Unwin, 1918. xlviii + 155pp. NLI. SPM/NUIM. Griffith's preface: pp. vii-xii, dated 21 March 1918.

Griffith, Arthur. *Songs, ballads and recitations*, edited by Piaras Béaslai. Dublin: Walton Musical Instrument Gallery (n.d.). 31pp. (*Songs, ballads and recitations by famous Irishmen*.)

Griffith, Arthur. 'The Novel of '98' *United Irishman*, 7 March 1903, p. 3. Signed: *Cuguan*.

Griffith, Arthur. 'The Oireaghias Ode'. *United Irishman*, 14 June 1902, p. 3. Signed: *Cuguan*.

Griffith, Arthur. *The resurrection of Hungary: a parallel for Ireland*. (A series of articles reprinted from the *United Irishman*.) Dublin: James Duffy; M.H. Gill & Son; Sealy, Bryers & Walker, 1904. 96p.p

Griffith, Arthur. *The resurrection of Hungary*. (Second edition.) Dublin: James Duffy and Co., 1904. 100pp. (Published on 16 December.) NLI, SPM/NUIM.

Griffith, Arthur. *The resurrection of Hungary, a parallel for Ireland; with appendices on Pitt's policy and Sinn Féin*. Third edition. Dublin: Whelan and Son, 1918. xxxii + 170pp. 3; portraits. This is the 'third edition' in the sense that 1904 series in the *United Irishman* was counted as the first edition. NLI, SPM/NUIM.

Griffith, Arthur. *The finance of the Home Rule bill: an examination*. Dublin: National Council, 1912. NLI.

Griffith, Arthur. *The Home Rule Bill examined*. Dublin: National Council (Sinn Féin), 1912.

Griffith, Arthur. *The Home Rule Bill examined*. Dublin, 1913.

Griffith, Arthur. 'The ignorant sister'. *United Irishman*, 26 April 1902, p. 3.

Griffith, Arthur. 'The influence of Fenianism'. In *In memory of O'Donovan*

Rossa, ed. by Sean MacGadhra. Dublin 1915, pp. 9-10.

Griffith, Arthur. 'The National Calendar for 1906'. *United Irishman*, 6, 13 and 20 January; 3, 10, 17 and 24 February; 3, 10, 24 and 31 March; 2 April 1906. All signed as *Cuguan*.

Griffith, Arthur. 'The return of Sinn Féin'. *Trace*, no. 4. Dublin, 1917.

Griffith, Arthur. *The 'Sinn Féin' policy. (A speech at the first Annual Convention of the National Council, 1905)*. 32pp. Dublin: James Duffy & Co.; M.H. Gill & Son, 1906. SPM Griffith Archives.

Griffith, Arthur. *The splendid silence. United Irishman*, 24 December 1904. Signed: *Cuguan*. Griffith comments upon Yeats' poem: 'How Ferencz Renyi kept silent'. NLI, SPM/NUIM.

Griffith, Arthur. *To rebuild a small nation*. Dublin, 1916. 7pp. Reprinted in 1918.

Griffith, Arthur. 'West British Art'. *United Irishman*, 18 March 1902, p. 6.

Griffith, Arthur. *When the Government publishes sedition: the census report on Ireland and the annual finance return*. Dublin: Irish Publicity League, 1915, 7pp. Reprinted in 1916.

Griffith, Arthur. 'William Rooney'. *United Irishman*, 10 May 1902, p. 3. Signed: *A.G.*

Works edited by (or on behalf of) Arthur Griffith

Griffith, Arthur, editor. Doheny, (Michael). *The felon's track ... or, History of the attempted outbreak in Ireland, embracing the leading events in the Irish struggle from the year 1843 to the close of 1848*. Original edition, with D'Arcy M'Gee's narrative of 1848, a preface (by Arthur Griffith), some account of the author's contemporaries. M.H. Gill & Son: Dublin, 1914. An index, and illustrations. xxxi 320pp. SPM/NUIM: 1918 Reprinted edition. The original edition was published in 1914. This is the third impression. The book has had six impressions, the best one being the 1951 impression.

Griffith, Arthur. *Economic salvation and the means to attain it; selected and arranged by Seamus Whelan*. Dublin: Whelan, 1911. 62pp. NLI, UCC.

Griffith, Arthur, editor. *Eire-Ireland*. Dublin, 26 October 1910-14. (The last annual was published in December 1914.)

Griffith, Arthur, editor. John Mitchel: *Jail journal ... with an introductory narrative of transactions in Ireland*. Original edition with a continuation of the journal in New York and Paris. Dublin: M.H. Gill & Son, 1921. A preface, appendices and illustrations; xlvii 463pp. Griffith's preface: pp. ix-xvi.

Griffith, Arthur, editor. *Leabhar na hÉireann. The Irish Year Book*, 1910; compiled by An Comairle Náisiúnta; the National Council. Dublin: Kevin T. Kenny, 1908, 1909, 1910, 1911.

Griffith, Arthur, editor. *Meagher of the sword; speeches of Thomas Francis Meagher in Ireland 1846-1848: his narrative of events in Ireland in July 1848, personal reminiscences of Waterford, Galway and his schooldays, edited by Arthur Griffith.* Dublin: M.H. Gill & Son, 1916. With a preface, appendices, index and illustrations. xxi 352pp. Griffith's preface: pp. iii-xviii. Note: Some copies of this work were dated '1917' which suggests a re-issue, but not another edition. NLI, SPM/NUIM.

Griffith, Arthur, editor. *John Mitchel, United Irishman: Jail journal.* Dublin, 1918. (Second edition)

Griffith, Arthur, editor. *Nationality* (a periodical), 19 June 1915-20 Sept. 1919. Dublin, 1915-19. LC. SPM/NUIM microfilm.

Griffith, Arthur editor. *Sinn Féin Weekly*, Dublin, May 1906-14. SPM/NUIM.

Griffith, Arthur, editor. 'The defeated address signed on behalf of the United National Societies Committee by Arthur Griffith and John D. Nugent'. *Sinn Féin Weekly*, 8 April 1911, p. 1.

Griffith, Arthur, editor. 'The National Council Fund by order of the National Council of Sinn Féin'. (Signed: John Sweetman, Arthur Griffith, Thomas Kelly.) *Sinn Fein Weekly*, 7 January 1911, p. 1; 15, 21 and 28 January, p. 1; 3 February, 1912, p. 1; and 2 March 1912, p. 2.

Griffith, Arthur, editor. *The poems and ballads of William Rooney.* Dublin: M.H. Gill, 1901. 203 pp. Ills. With Griffith's preface pp. ix-xi.

Griffith, Arthur, editor. *Thomas Davis* by John Mitchel. Dublin, 1914. 73pp. NLI, SPM/NUIM.

Griffith, Arthur, editor. *Thomas Davis: the thinker and teacher: the essence of his writings in prose and poetry.* Dublin, M.H. Gill & Son, 1914. SPM/NUIM, UCC. Reprinted in 1918. 288pp. Ills.

United Irishman. Dublin, March 1899-April 1906. Continued as *Sinn Féin* (weekly edition). SPM/NUIM.

WORKS ABOUT ARTHUR GRIFFITH

[Anon.] *Arthur Griffith: A study of the founder of Sinn Féin.* Dublin: Cahill & Co. (1919?). 24pp. On p. 3 of the pamphlet the title is given as: *A study of the originator of the Sinn Féin movement.* SPM Griffith's Archives.

[Anon.] 'Eire vajúdása'. *Pesti Napló*, 9 July 1937. 'Eire in labour' – a Hungarian account of the events leading up to de Valera's new Constitution, including the tenets of Griffith's *Resurrection*.

[Anon.] *Golden moments with Arthur Griffith.* Dublin: Whelan, 1917. 30pp. NLI.

Column, Padraic. *Arthur Griffith*. Dublin: Browne and Nolan, 1959. xvi + 400pp.

Cosgrave, W.T. 'Arthur Griffith', *Dictionary of national biography 1922-30*. London and New York: Oxford University Press, 1937, pp. 364-8.

Curran, C.P. 'Griffith, MacNeill and Pearse', in *Studies* 55 (Spring, 1966), pp. 21-8.

Davis, Richard. *Arthur Griffith*. Dublin: Dublin Historical Association, 1976. 48pp. (Irish History Series, no. 10).

Davis, Richard. *Arthur Griffith and Non-Violent Sinn Féin*. Dublin: Anvil Books, 1974. xxi +232pp.

Davis, Richard. 'Arthur Griffith, 1872-1922: architect of modernIreland', in *History Today*, 29/3 (1979), pp. 139-46 and 29/4, pp. 248-56.

Davis, Richard. 'Griffith and Gandhi: A study in non-violent resistance', in *Threshold* 3/2, (Summer 1959), pp. 29-44.

Ghall, Sean. *Arthur Griffith (and Michael Collins by Piaras Beaslai)*. Dublin: Martin Lester, 1923. 78 photos, 62pp.

Glandon, Virginia. *Arthur Griffith and the advanced nationalist press: Ireland 1900-1922*. New York: P. Lang, 1985. (4) + xi + (1) + 373pp.

Green, A.S. et al. 'Arthur Griffith' in *Studies* 44 (September 1922), pp. 337-55.

Kabdebo, Thomas. 'Ar ír-magyar párhuzam: Arthur Griffith történelmi forrásai'. *Századok* (1993), pp. 130-50.

Kabdebo, Thomas. 'Hungary and Ireland: historical contrasts, historical parallels'. (A lecture given in the Gallagher Art Gallery, 3 December 1991), Maynooth, 1992, 18pp.

Kabdebo, Thomas. *The Hungarian-Irish 'parallel' and Arthur Griffith's use of his sources*. Maynooth: St Patrick's College, 1988. 44pp.

Lyons, George A. *Some recollections of Griffith and his times*. Dublin: Talbot Press, 1923. (With a portrait), vii + 76pp.

McCartney, Donal. 'The Sinn Féin movement', in Kevin B. Nowlan (ed.), *The making of 1916*. Dublin: Browne and Nolan 1969, pp. 31-48.

Maye, Brian. *Arthur Griffith*. Dublin: Griffith College Publications, 1997. With photos, bibliog. and index. x + 403pp.

Maye, Brian. 'Why is it time for a new biography of Arthur Griffith', in *Études Irlandaises*, XVIII Sainghin en Melantois, France: Universités de Caen, Lille et Rennes II, December 1993, pp. 123-9.

McEvatt, R.M. 'Arthur Griffith and his early Sinn Féin policies', in *Capuchin Annual*, 1971, pp. 232-8.

McKenna, K.N. 'In London with the Treaty delegates', in *Capuchin Annual*, 1971, pp. 313-32.

O'Kelly, Seán. 'Arthur Griffith', in *Capuchin Annual*, 1966, pp. 132-50.

Ó Luing, Seán. *Art Ó Griofa*. Baile Átha Cliath: Sáirséal agus Dill, 1953. Ills. and facs., 429pp.

Ó Luing, Seán. 'Arthur Griffith 1871-1922: thoughts on a centenary', in *Studies* 60 (Summer, 1971), pp. 127-38.

Ó Luing, Seán. 'Arthur Griffith and Sinn Fein', in F.X. Martin (ed.), *Leaders and men of the 1916 Rising: Dublin 1916*. London, 1967, pp. 55-66.

Ó Luing, Seán. 'Ioldanacht Airt Ui Ghriofa', in *Comhar*. Baile Átha Cliath, Samhain, 1972, pp. 10-12 and p. 42.

Ó Mordha, Pilib. 'The Griffiths of Laurelhill, Co. Monaghan, and associated families', in *Clogher Record* 14/4 (1993), pp. 111-24.

Stephens, James. *Arthur Griffith: journalist and statesman*. Dublin: Wilson, Hartnell, 1922. (With a portrait.) 28pp.

Younger, Calton. *Arthur Griffith*. Dublin: Gill and Macmillan, 1981. 156pp. (Gill's Irish Lives).

Younger, Calton. *A state of disunion: Arthur Griffith, Michael Collins, James Craig, Eamon de Valera*. London: Muller, 1972. Ills. 349pp.

ARTHUR GRIFFITH AND HIS TIMES

Books, articles, government documents

Akenson, Donal Harmen. *The United States and Ireland*. Cambridge, Mass., 1973.

Beaslai, Piaras. *Michael Collins and the making of a new Ireland*. Dublin, 1926.

Beckett, James Camlin. *The making of Modern Ireland 1603-1923*. London, 1966.

Blake, Edward. 'Speech of the Hon. Edward Blake, M.P., for South Longford'. *Home Rule Bulletin* (New York) 2/4 (November 1894), Supplement, pp. 1-13.

Bourke, Marcus. *John O'Leary: a study in Irish separatism*. Tralee, 1967.

Bourke, Marcus. *The O'Rahilly*. Tralee, 1967.

Bowman, John. *De Valera and the Ulster question 1917-73*. Oxford, 1982.

Boyce, David George. *Englishmen and Irish troubles*. London, 1972.

Boyle, Andrew. *The riddle of Erskine Childers*. London, 1977.

Brasted, H.V. 'Irish nationalism and the British empire in the nineteenth century', in Oliver MacDonagh, W.F. Mandle and Pauric Travers (eds.), *Irish culture and nationalism, 1750-1950*. London, 1983.

Brennan, Robert. *Allegiance*. Dublin 1950.

Breuilly, John. *Nationalism and the State*. Manchester, 1982.

Brown S.J., Stephen 'The Dublin newspaper press: a bird's eye view, 1658-1916', in *Studies* 25 (March, 1936), pp. 109-22.

Carroll, F.M. *American opinion and the Irish question 1910-23*. Dublin, 1978.

Cinneide, Mairead Ni. *Marie de Buitleir: Bean Athbheochana*. Baile Átha Cliath, 1993.

Clarkson, J.D. *Labour and nationalism in Ireland*. New York, 1925.

Cody, Seamus; O'Dowd, John; Rigney, Peter. *The parliament of labour: 100 years of the Dublin Council of Trade Unions*. Dublin, 1986.

Colum, Pádriac. *The road round Ireland*, 1926.

Connelly O'Brien, Nora. *Portrait of a rebel father*. Dublin, 1935.

Coogan, Tim Pat. *Michael Collins*. London, 1990.

Coogan, Tim Pat. *De Valera: long fellow, long shadow*. London, 1993.

Copeland, Lewis and Lamb, Lawrence (eds.). *The world's greatest speeches*. New York, 1968.

Cosgrave, Art and McCartney, Donal (eds.). *Studies in Irish history presented to Robin Dudley Edwards*. Dublin, 1979.

Costello, Peter. *The heart grown brutal: the Irish revolution in literature from Parnell to the death of Yeats, 1891-1939*. Dublin, 1977.

Cox, Tom. *Damned Englishman: a study of Erskine Childers, 1870-1922*. New York, 1975.

Coxhead, Elizabeth. *Daughters of Erin*. London, 1965.

Coxhead, Elizabeth. *Lady Gregory: a literary portrait*. London, 1961.

Curran, C.P. 'Griffith, MacNeill and Pearse', in *Studies* 55 (Spring, 1966), pp. 21-8.

Curran, J.M. *The birth of the Irish Free State 1921-23*. Louisville, Alabama, 1980.

Curran, J.M. 'The issue of external relations in the Anglo-Irish negotiations of May-June 1922', in *Eire-Ireland* 3/1 (1978), pp. 15-25.

Czir, Sydney ('John Brennan'). *The years flew by*. Dublin, 1974.

D. *Ireland look into the mirror*. Dublin, 1916. (Tracts for Irishmen, No. 1.)

Dáil Éireann. 'Official Correspondence relating to the Peace Negotiations, June-September 1921'. Dublin, October, 1921, 28pp. SPM Griffith Archives.

Daly, M.E. *Industrial development and Irish national identity 1922-39*. Dublin, 1992.

Daly, M.E. 'Local government and the first Dáil', in Brian Farrell (ed.), *The creation of Dáil Éireann*. Dublin, 1994.

Dangerfield, George. *The damnable question: a study in Anglo-Irish relations*. London, 1977.

Davis, R.P. 'The advocacy of passive resistance in Ireland, 1916-22', in *Anglo-Irish Studies III* (1977), pp. 35-55.

Davis, R.P. 'Ulster Protestants and the Sinn Féin Press', in *Eire-Ireland* 15/4 (1980), pp. 60-85.

De Vere White, Terence. *Kevin O'Higgins*. London, 1948.

Doheny, Michael. *The felon's track*. Dublin, 1914.

Dwyer, Terence Ryle. *De Valera's darkest hour: in search of national independence 1919-32*. Dublin and Cork, 1982.

Dwyer, Terence Ryle. *Michael Collins and the Treaty: his differences with de Valera*. Dublin and Cork, 1981.

Edwards, Owen Dudley and others. *Celtic nationalism*. London, 1968.

Edwards, Owen Dudley. *The mind of an activist: James Connolly*. The centenary lecture delivered on 10 May 1968 under the auspices of the Irish Congress of Trade Unions in Liberty Hall. Dublin, 1971.

Edwards, Ruth Dudley. *Patrick Pearse: the triumph of failure*. London, 1977.

Ellis, Peter Beresford. *A history of the Irish working class*. London, 1972.

Ellman, Richard. *James Joyce*. New York, 1959.

Ellman, Richard. *The consciousness of Joyce*. London, 1977.

Fallis, Richard. *The Irish renaissance: an introduction to Anglo-Irish literature*. Dublin, 1978.

Fanning, Ronan. *Independent Ireland*. Dublin, 1983.

Farrell, Brian (ed.). *The creation of Dáil Éireann*. Dublin, 1994.

Farrell, Brian. *The founding of Dáil Éireann: parliament and nation-building*. Dublin, 1971.

Figgis, Darrell. *Recollections of the Irish war, 1914-21*. London, 1927.

Fitzgerald, Alexis. 'Erskine Childers', in *Hibernia*, 15 April 1977.

Fitzgerald, Desmond. *The memoirs of Desmond Fitzgerald, 1913-16*. London, 1968.

Flannery, J.W. *W.B. Yeats and the idea of a theatre*. New Haven and London, 1976.

Forester, Margery. *Michael Collins: the lost leader*. London, 1971.

Foster, R.F. 'Anglo-Irish literature, Gaelic nationalism and Irish politics in the 1890s', in J.M.W. Bean (ed.). *The political culture of modern Britain*. London, 1987.

Foster, R.F. *Modern Ireland, 1600-1972*. London, 1988.

Fox, R.M. *Green banners: the story of the Irish struggle*. London, 1938.

Fox, R.M. *James Connolly: the forerunner*. Tralee, 1946.

Fox, R.M. *Jim Larkin: the rise of the underman*. London, 1957.

Garvin, Tom. *The evolution of Irish nationalist politics*. Dublin, 1981.

Gaughan, J.A. *Austin Stack: a portrait of a separatist*. Dublin, 1977.

Gaughan, J.A. *Thomas Johnson, 1872-1963*. Dublin, 1980.

Gogarty, Oliver St John. *As I was going down Sackville Street*. New York, 1937.

Greaves, C.D. *Liam Mellows and the Irish revolution*. London, 1971.

Greaves, C.D. *The Irish Transport and General Workers Union: the formative years, 1909-1913*. Dublin, 1982.

Greaves, C.D. *The life and times of James Connolly*. London, 1961.

Greene, D.H. and Stephens, E.M. *J.M. Synge, 1871-1909*. New York, 1959.

Griffith, Kenneth and O'Grady, Timothy. *Curious journey: an oral history of Ireland's unfinished revolution*. London, 1982.

Gwynn, Stephen. *The student's history of Ireland*. Dublin, 1925.

Hancock, W.K. *A study of British Commonwealth affairs: problems of nationality 1918-36*. London, 1937.

Hayes, Michael. 'The importance of Dáil Éireann', in *Capuchin Annual*, 1969, pp. 336-9.

Henry, Robert Mitchell. *The evolution of Sinn Féin*. Dublin, 1920.

Hobson, Bulmer. *Ireland yesterday and tomorrow*. Tralee, 1967.

Holt, Edgar. *Protest in arms: the Irish troubles 1916-23*. London, 1960.

Hone, J.M. *W.B. Yeats 1865-1939*. London, 1942.

Hopkinson, Michael. *Green against green: a history of the Irish civil war*. Dublin, 1988.

Hyman, Louis. *The Jews of Ireland: from earliest times to the year 1910*. Shannon, 1972.

Jackson, T.A. *Ireland, her own: an outline of the Irish struggle for national freedom and independence*. London, 1946.

Jeffares, A. Norman. *W.B. Yeats: man and poet*. London, 1949.

Johnson, D.S. 'Partition and cross-border trade in the 1920s', in Peter Roebuck (ed.), *Plantation and Partition: essays in Ulster history in honour of J.L. McCracken*. Belfast, 1981.

Kain, R.M. *Dublin in the age of W.B. Yeats and James Joyce*. Newton Abbot, England, 1972.

Kállay, Miklós. 'A zöld sziget titka' ('The secret of the Green Isle'.) *Nemzeti Újság*, 1 December 1940. A Hungarian M.P. describing the Cromwellian massacres, the famine and the conditions leading up to Griffith's policies.

Kearney, Richard. *The Irish mind: exploring intellectual traditions*. Dublin, 1985.

Kee, Robert. *The bold Fenian men*. London: Quartet Books, 1976 and *Ourselves alone*. London, 1972; published in 3 volumes in 1976.

Kenny, H.A. *Literary Dublin: a history*. New York, 1974.

Kilroy, James. *The 'Playboy' riots*. Dublin, 1971.

Kotsonouris, Mary. 'The courts of Dáil Éireann', in Brian Farrell (ed.), *The creation of Dáil Éireann*. Dublin, 1994.

Laffan, Michael. *The partition of Ireland, 1911-25*. Dundalk, 1983.

Laffan, Michael. 'The Sinn Féin Party 1916-21', in *Capuchin Annual*, 1970, pp. 227-35.

Laffan, Michael. 'The unification of Sinn Féin in 1917', in *Irish Historical Studies*, 17 (March 1971), pp. 353-79.

Larkin, Emmet. *James Larkin: Irish labour leader 1876-1947*. London, c. 1965.

Lawlor, Sheila. *Britain and Ireland, 1914-23*. Dublin, 1983.

Lee, Joseph. 'Some aspects of modern Irish historiography', in Ernst Schulin (ed.). *Gedenkschrift Martin Gohing: Studien zur europaischen Gedichte*. Wiesbaden, 1968.

Lee, Joseph. *Ireland 1912-85: politics and society*. Cambridge, 1989.

Lee, Joseph (ed.). *Irish historiography, 1970-79*. Cork, 1981.

Lee, Joseph. 'The significance of the first Dáil', in Brian Farrell (ed.). *The creation of Dáil Éireann*. Dublin, 1994.

Levenson, Leah. *With wooden sword: a portrait of Francis Sheehy-Skeffington, militant pacifist*. Boston and Dublin, 1973.

Levenson, Samuel. *James Connolly: a biography*. London, 1973.

Loftus, R.J. *Nationalism in modern Anglo-Irish poetry*. Madison and Milwaukee, 1964.

Lynch, Patrick. 'Ireland since the Treaty', in T.W. Moody and F.X. Martin (eds). *The course of Irish history*. Dublin, 1967.

Lynd, Robert. *Galway of the Races: selected essays*. Dublin, 1990.

Lynd, Robert. 'The ethics of Sinn Féin', in *The Irish Year-Book/Leabhar na hÉireann*. Dublin, 1909, pp. 356-68.

Lyons, F.S.L. *Culture and anarchy in Ireland, 1890-1939*. Oxford, 1979.

Lyons, F.S.L. *Ireland since the Famine*. London, 1971.

Lyons, F.S.L. 'James Joyce's Dublin', in *Twentieth Century Studies* (November, 1970), pp. 14-24.

Lyons, J.B. *Oliver St John Gogarty: the man of many talents: a biography*. Dublin, 1980.

Lyons, J.B. *The enigma of Tom Kettle: Irish patriot, essayist, poet, British soldier, 1880-1916*. Dublin, 1983.

Macardle, Dorothy. *The Irish Republic; a documented chronicle of the Anglo-Irish conflict and the partitioning of Ireland, with a detailed account of the period 1916-23*. London, 1937.

Mac an Bheatha, Proinsias. *Tart na Cora; Séamus O Congháile, a shaol agus a shaothar*. Baile Átha Cliath, 1962.

MacBride, Maud Gonne. *A servant of the queen: reminiscences*. London, 1938.

McCarthy, Lawrence John. *The Irish question 1800-1922*. Louisville, Kentucky, 1968.

McCarthy, Donal. 'The political use of history in the work of Arthur Griffith', in *Journal of Contemporary History* 8 (January, 1973), pp. 3-19.

McCracken, D.P. *The Irish Pro-Boers, 1877-1902*. Johannesburg and Capetown, 1989.

MacDonagh, Oliver. *Ireland: the Union and its aftermath*. London, 1977.

MacDonagh, Oliver. *States of mind: a study of Anglo-Irish conflict, 1780-1980*. London, 1983.

MacLysaght, Edward. *Changing times: Ireland since 1898*. London, 1978.

MacLysaght, Edward. *Forth the banners go: the reminiscences of William O'Brien, as told to Edward MacLysaght*. Dublin, 1969.

Mansergh, N.S. *The Irish question 1840-1921: a commentary on Anglo-Irish relations and on social and political forces in Ireland in the age of reform and revolution.* London, 1940.

Maye, Brian. *Fine Gael 1923-1987: a general history with biographical sketches of leading members.* Dublin, 1993.

Middlemas, Keith (ed.). *Tom Jones: Whitehall Diary. Volume 3: Ireland 1918-25.* London, 1971.

Mitchel, John. *Jail journal.* Third impression (original edition with a continuation). Dublin, 1918.

Mitchell, Arthur. 'Labour and the national struggle', in *Capuchin Annual*, 1971, pp. 261-88.

Mitchell, Arthur. *Labour in Irish politics, 1890-1930: the Irish Labour movement in an age of revolution.* Dublin, 1974.

Mitchell, Arthur. 'The Irish Labour movement and the foundation of the State', in *Capuchin Annual*, 1972, pp. 362-74.

Moynihan, Maurice (ed.). *Speeches and statements of Eamon de Valera, 1917-73.* Dublin/New York, 1980.

Mulvey, H.F. 'Twentieth century Ireland', in T.W. Moody (ed.), *Irish historiography 1936-70.* Dublin, 1971.

Murphy, J.A. *Ireland in the twentieth century.* Dublin, 1975.

National Council of Sinn Féin. *The small nations.* Dublin, 1917.

Neary, Peter. 'The failure of economic nationalism', in *Crane Bag* 8 (1984), pp. 68-77.

Neeson, Eoin. *The civil war in Ireland, 1922-23.* Cork, 1966.

Norman, Edward. *A history of modern Ireland.* London, 1971.

O'Brien, J.V. *William O'Brien and the course of Irish Politics 1881-1918.* Berkeley, 1976.

O'Brien Connolly, Nora. 'The Pearse I knew', in *Hibernia*, 15 April 1977.

O Broin, Leon. *Revolutionary underground: the story of the Irish Republican Brotherhood 1858-1924.* Dublin, 1976.

O Broin, Leon. *The chief secretary: Augustine Birrell in Ireland.* Yale, Connecticut, 1970.

O'Casey, Sean. *Mirror in my house: the autobiographies of Sean O'Casey.* New York, 1956.

O'Connor, Frank. *The big fellow: Michael Collins and the Irish revolution.* Dublin, 1937.

O'Connor, Ulick. *A terrible beauty is born: the Irish troubles, 1912-1922.* London:, 1975.

O'Connor, Ulick. *Celtic dawn: a portrait of the Irish literary renaissance.* London, 1985.

O'Connor, Ulick. *Oliver St John Gogarty: a poet and his times.* London, 1964.

O'Donoghue, Florence. *No other law*. Dublin, 1954.

O'Hegarty, Patrick Sarsfield. *A history of Ireland under the Union*. London, 1951.

O'Hegarty, Patrick Sarsfield. *The victory of Sinn Féin: how it won it, and how it used it*. Dublin, 1924.

Ó Luing, Seán. *I die in a good cause: a study of Thomas Ashe*. Dublin, 1970.

O'Malley, Ernie. *The singing flame*. Dublin, 1978.

O'Neill, Marie. *From Parnell to de Valera: a biography of Jenny Wyse Power*. Dublin, 1992.

Ó Neill, Tomás P. agus Ó Fiannachta, Pádraig. *De Valera*. Baile Átha Cliath, 1968 agus 1970.

O Riain, Seán. 'Dáil Éireann, 1919', in *Capuchin Annual*, 1969, pp. 323-9.

Ó Síocháin, Séamas and Kabdebo, Thomas. 'Magyarország és a két Roger Casement'. *Századok* 1 (1994), pp. 135-41.

O'Sullivan, Donal. *The Irish Free State and its Senate: a study in contemporary politics*. London, 1940.

O'Sullivan, Seamus. *Essays and recollections*. Dublin, 1944.

O'Sullivan, Seamus. *The rose and bottle and other essays*. Dublin, 1946.

Ó Tuathaigh, M.A.G. 'Ireland 1800-1921', in Joseph Lee (ed.). *Irish Historiography, 1970-79*. Cork, 1981.

Pakenham, Frank (Earl of Longford). 'The Treaty Negotiations', in T.D. Williams (ed.). *The Irish struggle 1916-26*. London, 1966.

Pakenham, Frank (Earl of Longford). *Peace by ordeal: signature of the Anglo-Irish Treaty, 1921*. London, 1935.

Pakenham, Frank (Earl of Longford) and T.P. O'Neill. *Eamon de Valera*. London, 1970.

Ryan, Desmond. *James Connolly: his life, work and writings*. Dublin, 1924.

Ryan, Desmond. *Remembering Sion. A chronicle of storm and quiet*. London, 1934.

Ryan, Desmond. *Unique dictator: a study of Eamon de Valera*. Dublin, 1936.

Shiubhlaigh, Máire Nic. *The splendid years: the recollections of Máire Nic Shiubhlaigh as told to Edward Kenny*. Dublin, 1955.

Sibley, Mulford Quickert (ed.). *The quiet battle: writings on the theory and practice of non-violent resistance*. New York, 1963.

Skelton, Robin. *The writings of J.M. Synge*. London, 1974.

Smith, Des and Hickey, Gus. *A paler shade of green*. London, 1972.

Strauss, Emil. *Irish nationalism and British democracy*. Yale, Connecticut, 1951.

Taylor, Rex. *Michael Collins*. London, 1958.

Thompson, W.I. *The imagination of an insurrection: Dublin, Easter 1916: a study of an ideological movement*. New York, 1967.

Tierney, Michael. *Eoin MacNeill: scholar and man of action 1867-1945*. Oxford, 1980.

Townsend, Charles. *Political violence in Ireland: government and resistance since 1848*. Oxford, 1983.

The British campaign in Ireland 1919-21: the development of political and military policies. Oxford, 1975.

Valiulis, M.G. *Portrait of a revolutionary: General Richard Mulcahy and the founding of the Irish Free State.* Dublin, 1992.

Ward, A.J. *Ireland and Anglo-American relations 1899-1921.* London, 1969.

Ward, Margaret. *Maud Gonne: Ireland's Joan of Arc.* London, 1990.

Ward, Margaret. *Unmanageable revolutionaries: women and Irish nationalism.* Dingle, 1983.

Wilkinson, Burke. *The zeal of the convert: the life of Erskine Childers.* Washington, 1976.

Yeats, William Butler. *Dramatis personae 1896-1902.* London, 1936.

Yeats, William Butler. *Explorations.* London, 1962.

Younger, Calton. *Ireland's civil war.* London, 1968.

Arthur Griffith's Hungarian sources

Beust, Ferdinand. *Memoirs of Count Friedrich Ferdinand Beust.* London, 1887.

Boner, Charles. *Transylvania: its products and people.* London, 1865.

Deák, Ferencz. *A Hungarian statesman, a memoir.* London, 1880.

Delisle, Arthur. *Hungary.* London, 1914.

Görgey, Arthur. *My life and acts in Hungary.* London, 1852.

Gould, Warwick. 'How Ferencz Rényi spoke up ...', *Yeats Annual* 3 (1985), pp. 199-205.

Headley, Phineas Camp. *The authentic life of Louis Kossuth.* London, 1851.

Hengelmüller, Ladislas. Hungary's first for national existence, London, 1913.

Horváth, Mihály. *Huszonöt év Magyarország történetéből 1823-tól 1848-ig ... Második, javitott és bővített kiadás,* 2 köt. Pest, 1868.

Jókai, Mór. *Debts of honour.* London, 1900.

Jókai, Mór. *Hungarian sketches in peace and war.* Edinburgh, 1855.

Jókai, Mór. *Midst the wild Carpathians.* London, 1897.

Jókai, Mór. *The green book of freedom under the snow.* London, 1897.

Knatchbull-Hugessen, C.M. *The political evolution of the Hungarian nation,* vol. 1. London, 1908.

Kossuth, Lajos. *Memoirs of my exile.* London, 1880.

Klapka, György. *Memoirs of the War of Independence in Hungary.* 2 vols. London, 1850.

Leger, L. *History of Austria-Hungary.* London, 1889.

List, Friedrich. *The national system of political economy.* London, 1840.

Marczali, Henrik. *Übersicht der Geschichte Ungarns.* Budapest, 1918.

Paget, John. *Hungary and Transylvania with remarks on their condition, social, political and economical.* Second edition, London, 1850.

Patterson, Arthur J. *The Magyars: their country and institutions*. 2 vols. London, 1869.
Pesth Gazette (i.e. *Pesti Hirlap*).
Pulszky, Ferencz. *Mein Leben und Zeit*. Budapest, 1884.
Pulszky, Ferencz and Theresa. *Tales and traditions of Hungary*. 2 vols. London, 1851.
Pulszky, Theresa. *Memoirs of a Hungarian lady*. London, 1850.
Stiles, William H. *Austria in 1848-49*. 2 vols. New York, 1852.
Széchenyi, István. *Über dem Credit*. Leipzig, 1830.
Vámbéry, Arminius. *Hungary in ancient medieval and modern times*. London and New York, 1893.

APPENDIX

Titles of serials containing relevant material

Anglo-Irish Studies
Capuchin Annual
Claidheamh Soluis, An
Comhar
Cork Examiner
Daily Express
Dictionary of National Biography, 1922-30
Dublin Trade and Labour Journal
Éire-Ireland
Études Irlandaises
Evening Herald
Evening Press
Free State
Freeman's Journal
Gaelic American
Harp
Hibernia
History Today
Irish Bulletin
Irish Freedom
Irish Historical Studies
Irish Homestead
Irish Independent
Irish Labour Journal
Irish Nation and Peasant
Irish Press
Irish Statesman
Irish Times
Irish Weekly Independent
Irish Worker
Irish Worker and People's Advocate
Journal of Contemporary History
Leader
Liberator and Irish Trade Union
Magyar Hírlap
Magyar Nemzet
Nationality
Nemzeti Újság
New Statesman and Nation
Observer
Pesti Napló
Poblacht na hÉireann
Reynold's News
Scissors and Paste (London)
Sinn Féin (weekly and daily)
Southern Cross
Spark
Studies
Sunday Independent
Sunday Press
Sunday Times
Sunday Tribune
The Times

Index